ROUTLEDGE LIBRARY EDITIONS: LIBRARY AND INFORMATION SCIENCE

Volume 35

END-USER TRAINING FOR SCI-TECH DATABASES

END-USER TRAINING FOR SCI-TECH DATABASES

Edited by
ELLIS MOUNT

LONDON AND NEW YORK

First published in 1990 by The Haworth Press, Inc.

This edition first published in 2020
by Routledge
2 Park Square, Milton Park, Abingdon, Oxon OX14 4RN

and by Routledge
52 Vanderbilt Avenue, New York, NY 10017

Routledge is an imprint of the Taylor & Francis Group, an informa business

© 1990 The Haworth Press, Inc.

All rights reserved. No part of this book may be reprinted or reproduced or utilised in any form or by any electronic, mechanical, or other means, now known or hereafter invented, including photocopying and recording, or in any information storage or retrieval system, without permission in writing from the publishers.

Trademark notice: Product or corporate names may be trademarks or registered trademarks, and are used only for identification and explanation without intent to infringe.

British Library Cataloguing in Publication Data
A catalogue record for this book is available from the British Library

ISBN: 978-0-367-34616-4 (Set)
ISBN: 978-0-429-34352-0 (Set) (ebk)
ISBN: 978-0-367-43253-9 (Volume 35) (hbk)
ISBN: 978-0-367-43258-4 (Volume 35) (pbk)
ISBN: 978-1-00-300211-6 (Volume 35) (ebk)

Publisher's Note
The publisher has gone to great lengths to ensure the quality of this reprint but points out that some imperfections in the original copies may be apparent.

Disclaimer
The publisher has made every effort to trace copyright holders and would welcome correspondence from those they have been unable to trace.

End-User Training for Sci-Tech Databases

Ellis Mount
Editor

The Haworth Press
New York • London

End-User Training for Sci-Tech Databases has also been published as *Science & Technology Libraries*, Volume 10, Number 1 1989.

© 1990 by The Haworth Press, Inc. All rights reserved. No part of this book may be reproduced or utilized in any form or by any means, electronic or mechanical, including photocopying, microfilm and recording, or by any information storage and retrieval system, without permission in writing from the publisher. Printed in the United States of America.

The Haworth Press, Inc., 10 Alice Street, Binghamton, NY 13904-1580
EUROSPAN/Haworth, 3 Henrietta Street, London WCZE 8LU England

Library of Congress Cataloging-in-Publication Data

End-user training for sci-tech databases / Ellis Mount, editor.
    p. cm.
    "Has also been published as Science & technology libraries, volume 10, number 1, 1989"—T.p. verso.
    Includes bibliographical references.
    Contents: Introduction—Teaching controlled vocabulary and natural language to end-users of scientific online and CD-ROM databases / Christina A. Brundage—End-user searching in the corporate research setting: a planning assessment at Sandia National Laboratories / Linda J. Erickson, Nancy Jones Pruett—Promoting and supporting end-user online searching in an industrial research environment: a survey of experiences at Exxon Research and Engineering Company / Patricia L. Dedert, David K. Johnson—The role of medical libraries in end-user searching: teaching the MEDLINE database to health care professionals / Beryl Glitz—Courses for special librarianship offered in ALA accredited programs in 1987 and implications for the education of science/technology librarians / Constance M. Mellott—Sci-tech collections / Tony Stankus, editor—Information sources in supercomputing and supercomputers / Melvin G. DeSart—Sci-tech in review / Karla Pearce, editor—Sci-tech online / Ellen Nagle, editor—New reference works in science and technology / Arleen N. Somerville, editor.
    ISBN 0-86656-963-4
    1. Scientific libraries—Reference services—Automation—User education. 2. Technical libraries—Reference services—Automation—User education. 3. Technology—Information services—User education. 4. Science—Information services—User education. 5. Data base searching—Study and teaching. 6. Technology—Data bases. 7. Science—Data bases. 8. End-user computing. I. Mount, Ellis.
Z699.5.S3E525   1990
025.3'132—dc20
                                                                                                           89-27971
                                                                                                               CIP

End-User Training for Sci-Tech Databases

CONTENTS

Introduction	1
Teaching Controlled Vocabulary and Natural Language to End-Users of Scientific Online and CD-ROM Databases	3
Christina A. Brundage	
Introduction	3
To Teach Controlled Vocabulary or Not?	4
The Language of Science	5
Characteristics of Natural Language and Controlled Vocabulary	6
Characteristics of End-Users	9
Instruction in Use of Controlled and Natural Vocabulary	10
Conclusion	12
End-User Searching in the Corporate Research Setting: A Planning Assessment at Sandia National Laboratories	15
Linda J. Erickson	
Nancy Jones Pruett	
Introduction	15
Sandia Environment	16
Our Direction	23
Promoting and Supporting End-User Online Searching in an Industrial Research Environment: A Survey of Experiences at Exxon Research and Engineering Company	25
Patricia L. Dedert	
David K. Johnson	
Search for New Initiatives	27
Promoting End-User Searching	29

Structure of the Course	30
Follow-up to the Course	31
Public Search Terminal	32
Online Use	36
Continuing Support	43
Conclusions	44

The Role of Medical Libraries in End-User Searching: Teaching the MEDLINE Database to Health Care Professionals — 47
Beryl Glitz

Introduction	47
The Structure of Medline	48
Multiple Access to Medline	49
End-User Classes	52
End-User Training for Students	52

A *Chemical Abstracts* Training Seminar for Science Librarians — 55
Bruce Slutsky

I. Coverage and Organization of *Chemical Abstracts*	56
II. Use of Indexes	58
III. Online Searching of *Chemical Abstracts*	65

SPECIAL PAPER

Courses for Special Librarianship Offered in ALA-Accredited Programs in 1987 and Implications for the Education of Science/Technology Librarians — 77
Constance M. Mellott

Methodology	78
Courses in Special Librarianship	78
Courses for Specific Types of Special Libraries	82
Courses for Specific Types of Literature	83
Online Science/Technology Database Instruction	85
Field Work	86
Conclusion	86

SCI-TECH COLLECTIONS 89
Tony Stankus, Editor

Information Sources in Supercomputing and Supercomputers 91
Melvin G. DeSart

What Makes Them "Super"	91
Resource Tools	96
Monographs	97
Monographic Series	100
Conference Proceedings	101
Journals	103
Indexes and Abstracts	104
Online Databases	106
Research Centers	109

SCI-TECH IN REVIEW 111
Karla Pearce, Editor
Giuliana Lavendel, Associate Editor

SCI-TECH ONLINE 115
Ellen Nagle, Editor

Database News 115

NEW REFERENCE WORKS IN SCIENCE AND TECHNOLOGY 119
Arleen N. Somerville, Editor

Introduction

Searching of online databases has for many years been done chiefly by information professionals, such as librarians, information specialists and others with formal training in computerized retrieval. While there have long been a few organizations where a serious effort was made to encourage and train end-users to do their own searching, it has been only relatively recently that greater effort has been made to train end-users in the fine art (or science) of online searching. While law schools have for several years been turning out graduates who will expect to do online searching at their first jobs, this has not been nearly as common practice in science and engineering. In sci-tech disciplines efforts to increase collegiate end-user training and on-the-job training in searching are just beginning to be prevalent in a number of colleges and business/governmental organizations.

This issue is concerned with the training of end-users for online searching of sci-tech databases, done in a variety of environments. The first paper, by Christina A. Brundage, treats the subject from the standpoint of how to train end-users to search with both natural language and controlled vocabularies in the sciences. The paper points out the instances in which controlled vocabularies are more appropriate than natural language and vice versa. Linda J. Erickson and Nancy Jones Pruett describe a planning assessment for end-user searching at Sandia National Laboratories, including a test of the Dialog Corporate Connection.

Industrial research is the background against which the paper by Patricia L. Dedert and David K. Johnson is set. They relate how scientists at Exxon Research and Engineering Company have begun to do more online searching in response to the efforts made by the Information Center to encourage such activities. A specific area of end-user searching, the health care community, is addressed in the paper by Beryl Glitz, which emphasizes the role of MEDLINE. The activities of commercial vendors, the National Library of Medicine and medical libraries are described in regard to training end-users.

Training of science librarians at the New York Public Library's Science and Technology Research Center in the use of printed and online versions of *Chemical Abstracts* is discussed in the paper by Bruce Slutsky, a member of that staff. The paper includes a description of the training exercises used for the course. The special paper for this issue carries out the theme of library education, being a survey of courses at ALA-accredited library schools devoted to special librarianship, including those which deal with science and medical literature. It was written by Constance M. Mellott, who compares her findings with earlier surveys.

The special collection paper, prepared by Melvin G. DeSart, covers information sources on the subject of supercomputers and supercomputing. Following a brief historical review of the development of supercomputers, he cites and annotates both printed and online sources of information on these subjects. Following this paper are our usual features.

Ellis Mount
Editor

Teaching Controlled Vocabulary and Natural Language to End-Users of Scientific Online and CD-ROM Databases

Christina A. Brundage

SUMMARY. This paper reviews the similarities between scientific language and search language using controlled vocabulary or natural language. It discusses the nature of end-users in science libraries, types of information needs, and methods to teach the use of appropriate vocabulary.

INTRODUCTION

Academic and corporate science librarians in the United States and Canada have been teaching their patrons how to search bibliographic databases for several years. Stephen P. Harter has proposed the model of scientific inquiry as a useful way of viewing online searching,[6] and that model may appeal particularly to students and researchers in science. One aspect of searching, the use of controlled vocabulary, will be explored in this paper, with regard to parallels in the language of science. Scientists are familiar with controlled vocabularies in their disciplines, for example the naming of chemical compounds, geologic time-based classifications, and binomial nomenclature. In the mature sciences, such as mathematics,

---

Christina A. Brundage is Life Sciences Librarian at San Jose State University, Clark Library, One Washington Square, San Jose, CA 95192. Previously, she held a similar position at George Mason University in Fairfax, VA. She received her MSLS from Catholic University, Washington, DC and a Bachelor of Science degree in Natural Resources from Humboldt State University, Arcata, CA.

astronomy, basic medicine, and established areas of biology, vocabulary is part of received knowledge making up the paradigm of the discipline, and can be used as a model in teaching thesaurus use to novice end-user searchers of online and CD-ROM databases. This paper will emphasize the life sciences and use as examples Medline with its Medical Subject Headings (MeSH), and BIOSIS with the accompanying *BIOSIS Search Guide*. Search features of both online and CD-ROM systems will be discussed.

TO TEACH CONTROLLED VOCABULARY OR NOT?

In 1985, the Direct Patron Access to Computer-Based Reference Systems Committee of Machine-Assisted Reference Section of ALA's RASD promulgated objectives for end-user education, including this language:

> The user will understand the difference between free-text and controlled-vocabulary searching and will be able to determine which approach to use for the best search results.[4]

Although a search through the end-user literature reveals some recommendations to limit instruction to the use of natural language and free text, many studies and papers emphasize the need to teach the use of controlled vocabulary. Snow,[9] in discussing Medline instruction, strongly advises teaching sophisticated tools such as thesauri, tree structures, and other classification schemes. Haines[3] suggests proceeding from natural language to additional terminology through tracings in the descriptor fields of relevant references. In working with researchers at Exxon, Walton[10] states that, even with "routine" searching as the instructional goal, "some knowledge of sophisticated online techniques [such as the use of Registry Numbers] is required even for novices, if those techniques are critical to the effective searching of the database(s)." At the University of Ottawa, all major thesauri are placed beside the end-user search terminals (Janke[7]). Wannarka[11] recommends that patrons select appropriate MeSH terminology, even when their search will be run by an intermediary. Finally, Kirby and Miller[8] have found that successful use of thesaurus terminology is related to effective end-user search strategy, and principles of controlled subject access are considered a major component of Branch's[1] conceptual framework for teaching end-users.

THE LANGUAGE OF SCIENCE

With these exhortations to encourage even naive and infrequent searchers to use controlled vocabulary, science librarians have as an ally the language of science itself. Reports of scientific research are written in a framework of formal style and precise language either in order to allow other scientists to replicate the research or to build further research on the original report. A shared vocabulary is assumed. Ambiguity and imprecision of language are edited out. Often writers and researchers make use of hierarchical classification schemes, such as binomial nomenclature, classes of chemical compounds, or disease classifications. These hierarchies not only define individual concepts or entities within the structure, but also delineate relationships between the individuals. Both students and researchers in science are familiar with the use of classification and precise language. Librarians who instruct these scientists can make use of this fertile ground for the introduction of bibliographic database structure and thesauri. Snow[9] advises that in teaching novice searchers, "proceeding from the known to the unknown" is effective strategy. Science librarians can do just that by using parallels between scientific language or classification and thesaurus terminology or hierarchies.

However, not only is the language of science precise, but it is also living. Reports of research on the cutting edge may use many terms not found in even the latest scientific dictionary, terms familiar only to those within the field. "Immature" fields of science, without well-established paradigms and received knowledge, are especially prone to the proliferation of new vocabulary. Although the users of newly created terminology still strive for clarity and control, indexers and creators of thesauri cannot be expected to keep up, even if they publish new word lists annually. Acquired immunodeficiency syndrome was not a MeSH heading in 1981 when the literature began to be peppered with reports of the disease.

The changing nature of scientific language requires that we explain free text searching as well as controlled vocabulary to end-users. They tend to use the natural language of their field in search strategy anyway, but we must help them decide whether the employment of natural language or the use of controlled subject headings (or a combination of the two) is most effective.

CHARACTERISTICS OF NATURAL LANGUAGE AND CONTROLLED VOCABULARY

Many experienced searchers have an intuitive sense whether to use a subject heading or free text terminology in particular databases and for various types of search topics (Calkins[2]). End-users will not have that same insight, although they often possess a deeper intuition of the literature of their field than do intermediary searchers. Both insight into database structure and into the published research enhance searching ability. This type of intuition accrues with experience and practice, and cannot be taught in the two-hour to two-day workshops that the library literature indicates are typical end-user instruction sessions. However, there are several decision rules for choosing between controlled and free text terminology that should be clarified for end-users. Harter[5] has listed general attributes of natural language and controlled vocabulary. His excellent model suggests several ways in which the novice searcher can make decisions between these two types of subject searching. Thesauri are used for generic searches, for queries which match the specificity of controlled vocabulary, for unambiguous search questions, and when synonyms and homographs need to be controlled.

Generic searches are often of interest to scientists. These usually represent one concept of a complex Boolean strategy and are quite broad. Two examples are the reaction of any type of gastrointestinal disease to certain diet therapies and the zoogeography of a class of organisms. There are many types of gastrointestinal diseases and may be many individuals in the specified class; as such these are generic searches. Without a hierarchial thesaurus and indexing structure, they would be quite hard or impossible to complete. The Medline tree structures which allow for searching by broad subject can be compared to the *International Classification of Disease* two similar hierarchical lists. The online indexing of *Zoological Record* also allows for generic searches up and down the biological classification scheme without having to key in each individual species within the genus, family, order, class or phylum. Zoologists, already familiar with taxonomic classification, will appreciate this feature.

Teach the use of thesauri also when the controlled vocabulary matches the specificity and precision of the search request. Each thesaurus will encompass varying levels of specificity depending on how close a subject is to the central concern of the discipline. MeSH vocabulary is more specific in describing aspects of clinical medicine than in delineating terminology in the social aspects of health care. If end-users intend to search for only clinical subjects, MeSH may be adequate to describe their queries. "Huntington's chorea" and "thigh" are two narrowly-defined concepts. However, if searchers delve into the sociological aspects of medicine, they may be advised to use more natural language. Will the heading "Asian Americans" be precise enough, or will more specific free text terminology such as "Hmong" be needed?

Search concepts that are standardized, unambiguous or precise are more successfully represented by controlled vocabulary. These qualities have been discussed above as attributes of the mature sciences in which vocabulary has been established and precisely defined over time. Compared with the humanities or the social sciences (Wiberley[12]), the sciences are characterized by standardized, unambiguous language, reflected in both scientific literature and thesauri for scientific databases.

A problem with standard concepts in MeSH occurs when the National Library of Medicine changes or expands its headings each year, to remain current with the subjects and language of the literature. In the online version of Medline, when HTLV-III was changed to HIV, all retrospective records were changed to reflect the new terminology. Similarly, now that "epidemiology" has replaced "occurrence" as a subheading, online retrospective references can be found using the current subheading. The most current MeSH is the thesaurus of choice. However, with CD-ROM Medline, the older compact discs remain static and don't incorporate new terminology. A search for HIV must use either HTLV-III or HIV, depending on which year is searched, and the epidemiology of lyme disease is found under both occurrence and epidemiology subheadings, also depending on year. Which thesaurus should be taught to CD-ROM users of Medline? Which should be kept at the CD-ROM workstation? How can an end-user keep track of the changes in MeSH? Perhaps, until CD-ROM producers do yearly conversions of retrospective Medline years, free text searching may yield better results. The problem can be explained to end-users as a conflict between standardization and currency of scientific language.

Thesauri should be taught as sources of additional relevant terminology. The BIOSIS Search Guide's Master Index may suggest several additional keywords for concept searching, and MeSH often lists cross references to related terms. These serve as excellent sources for expansion and fine-tuning of search strategy. As a related aside, a thesaurus provides help with proper spelling, which all searchers find essential for retrieval!

A major function of vocabulary lists is the control of synonyms and homographs. Is cancer called "cancer," "tumors," or "neoplasms"? Is a "plant" an organism or a factory? The thesaurus gathers synonymous concepts under one approved term and defines terminology in its scope notes. End-users who are taught to consult thesauri are saved time thinking of and keying in synonyms, and spared the imprecision of undefined homographs.

Natural language is especially useful when new concepts are searched, when thesaurus terminology doesn't match search-topic specificity, when a scientific discipline itself is new, highly flexible or unstandardized, and when a highly comprehensive search is required.

New concepts may not be found as controlled vocabulary even in thesauri which are revised annually. These must be searched as free text from the title or abstract fields where new terminology will occur. End-users who are familiar with the scientific literature will be reminded of how new language enters and infiltrates their fields, eventually becoming accepted and widely understood.

Highly specific terminology also may be restricted to the natural language of title or abstract. For example, references to scientific instrumentation may be searched generically with subject headings, but a specific instrument may be mentioned only in an abstract.

Natural language may be a necessary adjunct to controlled vocabulary for a comprehensive search. Most end-users, however, seem to prefer high precision rather than high recall in their searches, referring exhaustive searches to intermediaries. For those end-users who want to conduct their own comprehensive searches, teach natural language as a complementary method to using thesaurus terminology.

CHARACTERISTICS OF END-USERS

End-users have varied information needs at different points in their careers. Undergraduates in science often are unfamiliar with the full complexities of their subjects, and may not yet know the range of terminology in their fields. Thesauri can be of great help to them in suggesting appropriate and related search language. As they progress in their education, contemplating the writing of theses and dissertations, students delve deeper into scientific literature and language, becoming familiar with the jargon and leading edge terminology of their topic. They are also likely to be familiar with print indices and abstracts which use controlled vocabulary. Consequently, they are often willing to use both natural and thesaurus language in their searches. Working scientists and researchers have less routine exposure to library tools such as indices, and more experience with the literature itself. They may resist the initial use of controlled vocabulary in favor of the terminology of their preferred journals. An instructor can point out the descriptors assigned to each bibliographic record in an effort to induce these people to expand their searching once an initial natural language search has produced some results. Some CD-ROM systems facilitate this search method by allowing a user to highlight individual parts of a bibliographic record such as subject headings. These can then be automatically searched without rekeying the terminology. Searchers can begin with natural language, highlight relevant headings, and painlessly expand the power of their search to controlled vocabulary.

Other differences among end-user searchers relate to the degree of expertise desired and the expected frequency of searching. End-users learn searching, not to attain another professional skill, but to obtain reference lists. Most do not want to become experts, nor do they search often enough to do so. The less skilled and infrequent searcher will be less inclined to learn how to use a thesaurus or search guide, and more apt to search in a quick and dirty fashion. He or she will rely on an intermediary to conduct complex searches, using the full range of expert abilities and tools.

INSTRUCTION IN USE OF CONTROLLED AND NATURAL VOCABULARY

Branch[1] proposes a conceptual framework for teaching end-user searching which includes how online searching fits into the entire information gathering process, the principles of database organization, search topic analysis, and evaluation of search results. Database organization encompasses indexing and controlled vocabulary. An introductory encounter should emphasize only one database and thesaurus as a model for searching in order to minimize information overload.

Beginning instruction in database organization should include an explanation of a typical record, with labelled fields. Emphasis should be placed on the difference between terms and phrases in the descriptor field(s) and words in the title and abstract fields. Their origin should be explored. Sometimes the author of the paper contributes all the terminology; alternatively indexers who are subject experts add the descriptor terms. The difference between searching for a string of letters as free text words, and searching for a concept in the descriptor field should be discussed. End-user searchers often believe that "the computer" searches for what they type in as concepts rather than as letters or symbols (Harter[5]). Only if they choose thesaurus terms, will they initiate a true concept search, because an indexer or author has intervened and assigned concept terminology to each reference. Searching free text will retrieve what is typed in letter by letter in exact order only. "AIDS" will retrieve AIDS only, not acquired immunodeficiency syndrome. Teaching this conceptual background is best done with plenty of examples from actual records!

Illustrations of appropriate thesaurus use can follow explanation of record structure. For example, MeSH can be used to illustrate correct terminology, see references, and cross references, although library jargon such as "see reference" should be avoided. Again, examples help illustrate points, and end-users can be encouraged to suggest topics and find appropriate subject headings.

Demonstrations of actual searches, comparing retrieval using free text and controlled vocabulary can illustrate when each method is most appropriate. For use of controlled language, the BIOSIS concept codes are excellent examples. A search in BIOSIS on the topic, "navigation or orientation in relation to magnetic fields" found several papers on orientation of bacteria, roots, and the spine to magnetic phenomena. The original requestor wanted references to migratory birds, and when the concept code for Animal Behavior was added to the search, the bacteria, roots, and spines dropped out.

If end-users have previously searched unsuccessfully for certain topics using natural language, redoing their searches as demonstrations can show the power of choosing appropriate thesaurus terminology. If done in a friendly and objective manner, answering the question, "Why didn't I find all those references?" can be quite instructive. In fact, some of the most receptive end-user students are those who have been slightly frustrated by their earlier search results. They know that they need to expand their search skills, in contrast to completely naive end-users who might think that conceptual instruction simply delays their opportunity to go online.

In another case, an end-user searcher was looking for the physiological aspects of "fight or flight" behavior. While the class of end-users felt they knew what "fight or flight" meant, they could find no MeSH term that came close enough. A free text search (interestingly enough, expressed "fight AND flight") revealed references with several different MeSH headings, such as "aggression," "defence mechanism," and "sympathetic nervous system." None were precise enough to use without encountering too many false drops; the natural language served best. In BIOSIS, most references found with "fight and flight" had the "behavioral biology" concept code, which was also much too broad to be used alone.

Teaching the rules of thumb for deciding when to use natural language versus thesaurus terminology should be followed by ample practice time with exercises designed to illustrate each method.

Two novice searchers working together can collaborate on strategy in a more productive manner than can one person working alone. After working with the database, searches should reconvene as a group to discuss their findings. The instructor often expands his or her knowledge of end-user needs and database capabilities based on issues and ideas which arise during these discussions. Flexibility, confidence, and willingness to learn are necessary traits when working with novice searches. Novices often have more confidence than beginning professionals (who may have been overexposed to the "mystique" of automated searching while in library school, and who may be worried about spending too much money in online time). Consequently, end-users often explore online more freely and the wise instructor stays open to what they learn. One end-user wanted to explore the concept "rotting logs" in relation to a certain insect group, and while the instructor was privately dubious of what might result, she encouraged his experimentation. To her surprise, almost all of the rotting log references were pertinent.

The follow-up discussion can also become a guided learning experience if exercises are designed well. Both instructor and end-users should remember that exercises serve as models of actual searches, and, as such, cannot reflect what might happen when a real-life search is done. Therefore, during practice time, end-users also should suggest and conduct searches for their work or classes, with feedback from the instructor.

CONCLUSION

Good models exist for differentiating between the use of natural language and controlled vocabulary, and many scientific databases have excellent controlled vocabularies such as MeSH and the BIOSIS concept codes. Furthermore, Harter's model of scientific inquiry as a metaphor for automated searching can be used to teach similarities between thesauri and scientific language. Although intuition and insight into database structure gained from long practice guide experienced searchers in terminology decisions, an introduction to controlled and natural language in science will enhance even the novice or infrequent searcher's ability to construct successful strategies. Basing the introduction on parallels in science and scientific language will strengthen the instruction.

BIBLIOGRAPHY

1. Branch, Katherine. Developing a conceptual framework for teaching end-user searching. *Medical Reference Services Quarterly*. 5(1): 71-75; 1986 Spring.
2. Calkins, Mary L. Free text or controlled vocabulary? *Database*. 53-67; 1980 June.
3. Haines, Judith S. Experiences in training end-user searchers. *Online*. 14-23. 1982 November.
4. Hamilton, Dennis. Library users and online systems: suggested objectives for library instruction. *RQ*. 25: 195-97. 1985 Winter.
5. Harter, Stephen P. *Online information retrieval: concepts, principles, techniques*. Orlando, FL: Academic Press; 1986.
6. Harter, Stephen P. Scientific inquiry: a model for online searching. *ASIS Journal*. 35(2): 110-117. 1984.
7. Janke, Richard V. Online after six: end-user searching comes of age. *Online* 15-29; 1984 November.
8. Kirby, Martha; Miller, Naomi. Medline searching on Colleague: reasons for failure or success of untrained end-users. *Medical Reference Services Quarterly*. 5(3): 17-34; 1986 Fall.
9. Snow, Bonnie. Making the rough places plain: designing Medline end-user training. *Medical Reference Services Quarterly*. 3(4): 1-11; 1984 Winter.
10. Walton, Kenneth R. Experiences at Exxon in training end-users to search technical databases online. *Online*. 42-50; 1983 Winter.
11. Wannarka, Marjorie B. A training program for the end-user in the academic health sciences center. *Medical Reference Services Quarterly*. 5(2): 95-101; 1986 Summer.
12. Wiberley, Stephen E. Jr. Subject access in the humanities and the precision of the humanist's vocabulary. *Library Quarterly*. 53(4): 420-433; 1983.

End-User Searching in the Corporate Research Setting: A Planning Assessment at Sandia National Laboratories

Linda J. Erickson
Nancy Jones Pruett

SUMMARY. A planning assessment for implementing end-user searching in a sci-tech research organization is presented. The special needs of a large, multidisciplinary research laboratory are appraised with emphasis on possible contributions by the Library's professional searcher group. A test of the DIALOG Corporate Connection is described, along with a consideration of possible costs and benefits to both the Technical Library and to the corporation.

INTRODUCTION

In recent years, library literature has included a growing number of articles dealing with "end-user" searching. Although this concept has existed since online systems first became publicly available, it is only in the late 1980s that end-user searching has become feasible due to a variety of factors such as lower cost, ease of use, and improved equipment capabilities. Corporate libraries, espe-

---

Linda J. Erickson is Technical Information Specialist at Sandia National Laboratories, Technical Library, Division 3144, Albuquerque, NM 87185. She has a BS in biology from the University of Wyoming and an MA in librarianship from San Jose State University.

Nancy Jones Pruett is Supervisor of Archives and Records Management at Sandia National Laboratories, where she was previously Technical Information Specialist. She has a BA in geology from Rice University, an MLS from Texas Women's University, and an MBA from Southern Methodist University.

This work was supported by the U.S. Department of Energy under Contract DE-AC04-76DP00789.

© 1990 by The Haworth Press, Inc. All rights reserved.

cially in sci-tech organizations, have lagged somewhat in implementation of end-user searching because they have professional searchers on staff who have traditionally filled the organization's literature search needs. This lag contrasts sharply with the normally "proactive" approach of sci-tech librarians who are generally in the forefront of new developments and in adoption of new technologies.

SANDIA ENVIRONMENT

Sandia National Laboratories is a large, multiprogram engineering organization with responsibility for national security programs in defense and energy. Sandia employs about 7200 people in Albuquerque, of whom 2944 are Members of Technical Staff (MTS). These scientists and engineers perform research in a variety of scientific disciplines, so the Technical Library must support a wide diversity of subject interests.

The Technical Library at Sandia has always had a group of Technical Information Specialists with assigned responsibilities for literature searching. The Library budget includes monies for online searches (up to a certain amount), and anyone within the corporation can request a job-related literature search. The obvious question then becomes, "Why even worry about end-user searching?"

The primary reason is that our librarians have always been proactive in seeking out new techniques to provide better, more efficient service to our scientists and engineers and have generally been successful in gaining management support for new ventures. For the past several years we have been interested in supporting end-user searching, but have been uneasy about the idea of "turning people loose" to do their own searching without prior planning and organized implementation. This would be a disservice to both the Technical Staff and the corporation as a whole.

Additionally, in recent years, there have been a small but increasing number of MTSs who have expressed some interest in doing their own computerized literature searching. Factors contributing to this increased interest may include direct marketing of online services to scientists in professional journals, use of online search services during professional education, and such mundane factors as greater distances from Sandia's new research buildings to the Library.

Past Experience with End-user Searching

End-user searching is not a new concept at Sandia; during the past ten years the Library has trained a number of scientists and engineers to use various online systems. In 1976, the Library had a public access terminal to the DOE/RECON system, and RECON'S demise was loudly lamented. For a number of years, we have had some chemists doing their own chemistry searches on ORBIT, and now STN. The Technical Library's online catalog, DOBIS, has been available within the Library building for more than five years.

Throughout the Laboratories, widespread use is made of the Sandia Computing Network. Last year DOBIS was made available through this computing network for individual office access. In April 1988 the final test group for "DOBIS from Your Desk" rated remote access to journal literature as the next major step, so we began a more formal feasibility study.

Possibilities Considered for Journal/Report Access

The Library has been monitoring developments in end-user searching for several years, including tests of In-Search and Easy-Net. The Sandia feasibility study of providing remote online access to Technical Staff was completed in June 1988. This study concentrated on the three alternatives that seem to be our best possibilities for offering journal and report access:

1. Purchase and mount database tapes on the Library's IBM4381 computer;
2. Purchase CD-ROM products to provide access;
3. Allow users to search online databases, either through the search services used by our professional searchers or through one of the end-user-oriented front ends or gateways.

Each of these alternatives is discussed in further detail.

1. *Purchase and mount database tapes on the Library's IBM4381 computer*. A number of database producers generate magnetic tapes containing their indexing and abstracting information. Our interest

in this option was triggered by an article about the Georgia Tech Library by Miriam Drake.[1] Georgia Tech mounted tapes from Information Access Co. and INSPEC on their IBM4381 computer and allowed remote searching of them using the same search software (BRS Search) as used for their online catalog. This would seem to be an ideal situation since users would have to be trained in only one search system for both internal and external information.

While no one database producer's subset matches our library collection or our users needs exactly, INSPEC is our most heavily used database for search requests and its journal list is comparable to our most-used journals, so we centered our investigations on INSPEC. We also checked costs on COMPENDEX and ISI tapes to see how they compare.

At the time of the study, a current subscription to INSPEC tapes cost $18,600 for the most recent year, with a maximum of 50 hours of in-house searching and 100 SDI profiles. Earlier tapes are cheaper, however, so we could have have gotten a five-year set for about $55,000. Our current searching of INSPEC (which covers more than five years, of course) does not equal that amount. COMPENDEX's costs were about the same for a five-year set, and ISI's costs were considerably higher without the inclusion of abstracts.

We decided not to pursue this option because the tape cost would be augmented significantly by the necessary purchase of search software (our current DOBIS software is not suited to this application). We also felt that it would be a compromise in terms of service since we could only offer five years of one database, and Sandia's needs are scattered across many different subject disciplines. (We may reconsider this option at some time in the future, e.g., if privacy of our search requests becomes a more driving issue, or if the search volume builds to significantly more than the tape and software costs, or if we get a new search system to handle our internal Library catalog.)

2. *Purchase CD-ROM products to provide access*. At the time of the feasibility study, there was considerable excitement about CD-ROM, with emerging products aimed at the end-user. A recent *Library Technology Reports*[2] on "Optical Media for Libraries" listed about 25 products with journal indexes on CD-ROM. However,

most cover subject areas which are inappropriate for us or cover only a very small subset of a large database such as NTIS (our second most-highly-used database). Also, CDs have only enough space to store one or two years of a major journal index with abstracts, so a retrospective search would require changing disks several times. To accommodate remote and/or multiple users, a "juke box" device would be required, and these are just beginning to come on the market.

Another significant consideration is that each CD-ROM product from a different vendor has different search software, thus creating a severe training and support problem. Our conclusion was that CD products might be considered as replacements for the Library's printed indexes and abstracts, but it did not appear feasible at this time to try to use them for remote journal searching by end-users.

3. *Allow users to search online databases, either through search services used by our professional searchers or through one of the end-user-oriented front ends or gateways.* A proliferation of products designed to provide a front end or user-friendly interface have been appearing in recent years, and the major online search services have made available low-cost, after-hours access to selected databases. Literature was gathered and studied on EasyNet, Knowledge Index (from DIALOG), BRS After Dark, BRS Colleague, STN Express, DIALOG Business Connection, and DIALOG Medical Connection. However, none of these seemed to be quite the right solution for our particular environment.

Through colleagues, we discovered that AT&T Library Network Services was in the midst of testing a pilot program to provide online access to end-users through DIALOG Corporate Connection (DCC), a menu-driven system with access to 85 sci-tech and business databases (similar in structure to the DIALOG Business and Medical Connections). Based on preliminary investigations, it appeared that DCC would better meet our needs than any of the other alternatives we had considered.

The recommendation from our feasibility study was to set up a Sandia test of the DIALOG Corporate Connection similar to the test taking place at AT&T Bell Laboratories.

Dialog Corporate Connection Test Project

During the month of August 1988, DIALOG issued passwords and sent us sample documentation for a Test Group of fourteen technical users. The group was selected from among volunteers who already were familiar with modems and communication software (so that we could minimize technical start-up problems). Users were given no training in order to see if training was necessary. They were told to assume that costs would be about $110 per hour of connect time and were asked to evaluate the system as though the costs were being charged back to them.

Eleven of the fourteen users said they would want the service. Two of the remaining three said they preferred to use the Reference Librarians (both had offices located in close proximity to the Library). The third person did not find what he was looking for and did not have time to get help.

A wide variety of terminals, telecommunication packages and modems was tested, and the users did have some trouble getting set up since the documentation did not accurately describe the parity, stop bits, etc. Only two users demonstrated any indication of having read the documentation beyond the logon procedures; the rest seemed able to use the system once they got to the first menu. What users liked most about DCC was the wealth of information available and the flexibility of doing the searches themselves. However, they had trouble knowing which database to search, they felt it was slow, and they wanted a number of specific changes that we passed on as suggestions to DIALOG. Many of them also had trouble with what they called "inconsistent terminology," e.g., CAD versus Computer Aided Design, or the way author's names are handled (initials versus full names). These problems are only too familiar to any professional searcher.

When we asked the Test Group to estimate the number of Sandians who would want the service in order to see how their estimate compared with ours, they estimated between 10% to 25% of the Technical Staff (or 294 to 736 people). Since the Library currently has about 350 people with passwords to DOBIS, our online catalog, we felt 400 people was a reasonable estimate of the number who would want to use the service.

Based on test results, we decided it was worth trying to work out the internal procedures for a true pilot project, including charge back of costs and establishment of training programs and help with hardware and search software difficulties. This next phase has been on hold during some staffing changes and reorganization of responsibilities within the Library's Reference Division.

Potential Benefits of Large-Scale End-User Searching

We know from studies of scientists' literature use that the journal literature is a valuable tool to our users. The Library has already invested considerable monies in our journal and report collections, and we feel that providing increased access to the contents of these collections is an important value-added service.

One of the most exciting possibilities of end-user searching is the potential to fill unmet needs for information. The Test Group said that 51% of the time they searched for information they would not have "bothered" the Library about. In his comments, one user said that when information is rapidly accessible, questions start being asked which otherwise would be ignored (by researchers). He indicated that many of his coworkers would not have gone to the reference library even though they did have questions. Whether it is a matter of remote location, reluctance to ask for help, or inability to describe research needs to a search intermediary, it is clear that many in the DCC Test Group found information with DCC that they would not have found otherwise. The Test Group even included one researcher who did not know the Library would do searches for him.

There also would be cost-related advantages for the Library in providing DCC. For example, if end-user searching were to reach the projected level (with an estimated average of about $300 per year per user), Sandia's volume discount on DIALOG would increase, thus reducing the Library's per hour cost. By establishing a group contract instead of each end-user having to do so, the Library would provide accounting efficiencies and save money for the corporation.

The Library's search requests have increased an average of 6% per year in the past three years, and we have no reason to expect the volume to level off. It is possible that end-user searching would reduce the number of routine searches coming to our professional searchers and also would provide us with a more sophisticated and knowledgeable search requester for those questions that do come to us. However, we expect that staff time spent helping end-users would easily make up for any decrease in searches that might occur. A more subtle benefit might be a heightened corporate awareness of the complexities of information retrieval and of the Library's significant contribution to the total research effort.

Potential Costs and Concerns

In spite of the many potential benefits of end-user searching, we must, as responsible professionals, consider the total costs to the corporation of implementing large-scale end-user searching. The most obvious of these is the significant increase in direct costs for external contracts plus the not-insignificant cost of highly-paid scientists' time. Less obvious are the probable increases in the Library's workload in the form of overseeing online contracts, password assignment and control, and performing or managing charge back of online search costs.

One of the largest costs to the Library is the whole spectrum of "knowledge consultant" activities needed to support the end-user: publicity, training, troubleshooting, provision of a Help Desk function. It would be truly irresponsible for us to raise end-users' expectations without being able to support them in utilizing online search capabilities as efficiently as possible.

We also need to maintain our hard-won researcher-librarian bridge so that we can tactfully supplement end-user searches with more in-depth, professional searches when necessary. If we can establish a comfortable partnership which utilizes both the researcher's technical knowledge and our online expertise, corporate research efforts will be advanced.

Another "cost" that must be considered is the potential of

changes to the library's existing paper flow. Most library processes are still based on pieces of paper, and recent years of dealing with offline printouts from computerized databases have enabled libraries to hone their document fulfillment capabilities. But a large migration to end-user searching of electronic information could put us back into the era of incomplete citations and transposed numbers unless we can find ways to incorporate electronic ordering into the end-user search process.

OUR DIRECTION

As previously mentioned, our Library plans to set up a true pilot project using DIALOG Corporate Connection within the next several months. If the project meets our expectations, we hope to be able to make end-user searching generally available to our Technical Staff by late 1989.

Obviously, between then and now, we have many concerns and details to resolve. We will continue to seek better ways to provide end-user support as technological advances create new opportunities. As the resident source of professional search knowledge, we have much to offer the corporate research effort.

REFERENCES

1. Drake, Miriam A. Library 2000 Georgia Tech: a glimpse of information delivery now and in the year 2000. *Online*. 11(6): 45-48; 1987 November.
2. Boss, Richard W.; Harrison, Susan B. Optical media for libraries. *Library Technology Reports*. 23(6): 783-896; 1987 November-December.

Promoting and Supporting End-User Online Searching in an Industrial Research Environment: A Survey of Experiences at Exxon Research and Engineering Company

Patricia L. Dedert
David K. Johnson

SUMMARY. Scientists at Exxon's basic research facility have been offered the opportunity to learn the basics of online searching of STN databases. A growing number of scientists have their own IDs and search for themselves in their offices. Scientists also have access to menu-driven searching using SearchMaster scripts and the Guided Search feature of STN Express software on a public terminal. End-user searching (of STN, DIALOG, and ORBIT databases) has been slowly increasing. New avenues of supporting and promoting these efforts are explored.

The research personnel at Exxon's basic research facility in Clinton, New Jersey, need technical information in a number of fields:

Pat Dedert is Staff Chemist and Group Head of Technical Searching at the Clinton Information Center of Exxon Research and Engineering Company, U.S. Route 22 East, Clinton Township, Annandale, NJ 08801. She has a BS in Chemistry from Bucknell University and MS and PhD degrees in Inorganic Chemistry from Northwestern University.

David Johnson is Staff Chemist and technical searcher at Exxon Research and Engineering Company's Clinton New Jersey Information Center. He has a BS in Chemistry from the University of Toledo, an MA in Organic Chemistry from Princeton University, and is working on his dissertation for a PhD in Information Science at Rutgers University.

chemistry, physics, biology, petroleum processing, and energy resources, to name but a few. To get the information they need, the scientists have access to the services of experienced technical searchers with advanced degrees in chemistry. Researchers can request "quick and dirty" searches, detailed state-of-the-art analyses, and anything in between. In addition, some Exxon researchers prefer to be able to do at least some of their own searching, and our goal is to assist them in learning and using online resources.

Increasing computer literacy and the widespread availability of personal computers are undoubtedly important reasons for the growing desire of scientists to do their own searching. At our location there is another important factor, however: the information center is housed in a completely separate wing of the building, a good five-minute walk from our clients' offices. Telephone requests, particularly when the explanation requires a structure or diagram, can be frustrating. Some of our scientists are understandably eager to save time and inconvenience by making good use of their office PCs.

End-user searching at other companies has been discussed in the literature,[1,3-5,8] and Exxon's early experiences in promoting end-user searching have also been described.[2,6,7] Our experiences include experiments with a computer-mediated training and search system (Drexel University's IIDA),[2] delivery of training courses tailored to the needs of small research groups,[7] and development of menu-driven search "scripts" using SDC's SearchMaster software.[6] The SearchMaster scripts were made available on a publicly accessible PC in our information center; several end users also used the SearchMaster scripts on their own PCs.

In addition, for a number of years we have assisted highly motivated end users by advising them on the choice and setup of searching hardware, telecommunications software, and the choice of online system; by providing passwords and system documentation for them; and by handling monthly invoices (billing all costs to the client).

Throughout this period, we also actively promoted end-user searching of our in-house, proprietary databases on our mainframe computer system (using a purchased version of ORBIT software), through half-day training courses and the development of a menu-driven search system. Thereby, searchers of the in-house system get a good introduction to the commands and search process encountered in commercially available databases.

Despite these efforts, we became aware in 1988 that some of our clients perceived us as obstructing end-user searching because we did not more visibly offer training and assistance. It had indeed been several years since we had run a new campaign or introduced a new search system. Our SearchMaster setup, while still used with satisfaction by a number of clients, had limitations frustrating to many. During this same period there was also an increase in the number of requests from end users for their own searching passwords. We decided that it was time to reexamine goals with regard to end-user searching and to find a better way to meet those goals.

SEARCH FOR NEW INITIATIVES

We first wanted to examine our own philosophy of end-user searching. In the early days, we felt strongly that end users should be protected from the possibility of incomplete retrieval or bad data. Thus, fairly detailed training courses seemed necessary. However, some of our end users apparently perceived strong cautionary warnings and detailed explanations of file structures and searching subtleties as the intermediary's attempt to protect turf, rather than as a legitimate concern for their welfare.

Subsequent experience has shown us that most end users are *not* trying to do their own patent novelty searches and that they neither need nor want to be trained as professional searchers. Many end-user searches are for articles by known authors or for a few references in an area of new research interest. Many end users do call on the professional searchers when they get into trouble with either too few or too many references.

We know that we cannot keep end users out of online databases, even if we want to, any more than we would keep them from doing their own searches in printed *Chemical Abstracts* (*CA*). In order to gain trust and foster better client-searcher relationships, we decided to soft-pedal our cautionary warnings about the types of searches an end user should or should not do and to keep training simple. We also decided to be more visible in our offers to assist the clients in doing their own online searching, knowing that if they could look on us as allies in their attempts to find their own information, they might more readily call on us when their efforts proved unsatisfactory.

We wanted our new end-user searching initiative to make it as easy as possible for the end user to get started in online searching. Our early experiences had taught us that all but the most motivated end users are easily frustrated by the complexities of online searching. They are confused by the many choices of online vendors. They seldom care about the internal structure of databases like *CA*. Their use is sometimes so infrequent as to make it difficult to remember even a few basic search commands.

In order for us to remove the burden of decision-making from our clients, we wanted to recommend just one online system. After consideration, STN International was the system we chose. STN offers nearly all of the databases of current and potential interest to our clients (with the current exception of ISI's SCISEARCH). Our clients most often need the *CA* database (see Tables 2 and 4), and STN is the only online source of *CA* abstracts, a very important factor in our decision.

Another important consideration was the availability of the new search software STN Express, with its Guided Search menus for use by those unfamiliar with search commands. We found Guided Search to be much more flexible and user-friendly than our existing SearchMaster scripts. As a PC software package, Express has many nice features not available in an online menu system such as DIALOG's Medical Connection.

We also thought that STN's training options were varied and flexible; as well as traditional training courses, the inexpensive STN MENTOR tutorial disks and the free booklet *Getting Started in CAS ONLINE* make self-training a viable option. We thought our clients would appreciate the fact that all STN commands can be used in a novice mode, which prompts the user to supply necessary parameters. In addition, we thought that the availability of expert help from chemists at the STN Search Assistance Desk was an important benefit.

A final consideration was the ease of obtaining multiple STN passwords for our end-user population. STN is willing to provide as many passwords as we need and to incorporate those accounts under our central billing umbrella. Therefore, we need to handle only one bill each month, rather than multiple bills. Also, each end user on our account can receive all applicable discounts.

PROMOTING END-USER SEARCHING

Once we decided upon STN as the vendor to recommend to our clients, we had to decide how to promote the system and which training options to make available; again, we did not want to offer the clients too many confusing options. Should we recommend that everyone purchase a copy of STN Express? At about $550 per copy, this recommendation might frighten off many users not sure of their commitment to searching. Also, the high cost of Express might only be justified to those who need its more sophisticated features, such as off-line creation of (sub)structures for searching and the merge of text and graphics. We did not know whether we could, in conscience, recommend the purchase of Express to the majority of our users, most of whom do not need graphics because they are generally dealing with reactions of petroleum streams. In addition, many of our clients use non-IBM workstations, which do not support Express. Nonetheless, principally because of Guided Search, we leaned toward recommending Express, particularly to chemists and those who did not already have telecommunications software.

At this point in our deliberations we were greatly helped by a committee of client scientists who were already end-user searchers. The committee firmly believed in the desirability of offering a low-risk, low-investment opportunity to become familiar with the basics of online searching. They were impressed with the capabilities of the STN Express software, but felt that it was too expensive for mass recommendation, especially since many client offices already had telecommunications software. They believed that simple command searching would not discourage end users and thought that a number of users would be willing to use self-instructional materials.

The committee thought a one- or two-hour course on fundamental skills, emphasizing basic search commands, would be well received and would be an effective introduction to searching. After taking the course, interested clients would be given passwords and system documentation. Those who wished to purchase Express could do so, with the experiences of the course to help them decide.

Our STN account representative offered to develop and deliver a short course in the basics of the STN system, concentrating on the *CA* and Registry Files. He also offered to guide each participant through a half-hour, online practice session after the course. This left us with the relatively easy task of advertising the course and scheduling the individual practice sessions.

We sent to each scientist at our location course invitations consisting of a one-page letter entitled, "Online Searching on Your Own PC." The letter emphasized that it is rather easy to learn the four basic commands necessary to do simple searches, and pointed out that many researchers are already equipped with the necessary hardware and software.

Enclosed with each invitation was an STN promotional booklet listing available databases. We also enclosed our own four-page summary of the preliminary requirements for getting started in online searching, including short descriptions of hardware, software, and training options.

Our initial invitations went to approximately 150 people; about 25 scientists responded and 14 of these actually attended. A number of those unable to attend requested a make-up session as soon as possible. When the make-up session was given a month later, 22 people attended. Over 90% of the attendees did come to an individual practice session the same afternoon or the following day.

STRUCTURE OF THE COURSE

The tutorial session took about 1-1/2 hours, and covered the following topics:

1. Evolution of literature from primary journals to secondary sources and online databases;
2. Scope of the *CA* and Registry Files;
3. Format of STN commands;
4. Basic commands: FILE, EXPAND, SEARCH, and DISPLAY;

5. Truncation and character-masking symbols;
6. Boolean & Proximity Operators: AND, OR, NOT, (L), (A), and (W);
7. Refining a search by use of proximity operators; limiting retrieval to articles by a particular author or company;
8. Finding Registry Numbers by matching a name or synonym; and
9. Using Registry Numbers to search File *CA*.

Examples of online search interactions were presented in the slides and handouts, but no online demos were given in the lecture portion of the course. Handouts included copies of all slides shown in the course, database summary sheets for Files *CA* and Registry, STN price lists, and STN Pocket Guides.

At the individual, 30-minute practice sessions the students were permitted to try a real search in their field, guided by the STN instructor.

FOLLOW-UP TO THE COURSE

A single survey was sent to all participants three months after the first course (two months after the second). Twenty-five (69%) of the 36 attendees responded. The purpose of the questionnaire was three-fold: to determine the level of satisfaction with the course format, to find out how many of the participants had searched since taking the course, and to learn why they had or had not searched. About 80% of the responders thought the course was just about right in length and level of detail presented—and would recommend the course to their colleagues.

Of interest, however, was the response to the question "Did you learn what you wanted to learn?" Forty-two percent of the respondents said "somewhat" instead of "yes," and one person said "no." From the "no" comments received, it appears that some had wanted to learn how to search for compounds by structure. Many of those who responded "somewhat" would have appreciated more practice time to gain confidence in their searching skills; they seemed unsure that their knowledge would stay with them through the periods when they do not do any searches.

Suggestions to improve the course included more practice time, inclusion of online demos in the lecture, and a follow-up session a few weeks after the course to reinforce the teachings. One person suggested a "slower" course, while another would have preferred a higher level course for more serious searchers. Again, a few people want to learn to search for compounds by structure. About 80% think that more training may be needed in the future, especially in the basics of STN and/or the *CA* File.

Nine of the respondents (36%) said that they had done some online searching since the time of the course, most of these doing between two and five searches; one person had searched more than 10 times. All of these people were either satisfied or very satisfied with the results of their own searches. Three of the people who had searched said that they used the STN Express Guided Search menus instead of command searching for at least some of their searches.

We asked those who had searched how they would have found their information prior to the course: 41% would have done the search themselves using printed materials; 27% would have done without the search; only 32% would have asked a professional searcher to do the search. This reinforces our belief that a certain number of our clients are either very reluctant to ask for assistance in finding their information or they prefer to search for themselves in most circumstances, even if they have to do so by manual methods.

The reasons most often cited for not doing any searching were "no time" and "no need." A few people expressed the feeling that the course had taught them that the searches they most often need are too complex or involved for them to do themselves.

PUBLIC SEARCH TERMINAL

Until 1988, when the number of end-user IDs increased markedly, the mechanism for most end-user searching at our Clinton research center was a publicly available PC. Its use continues even with increased personal IDs. Feedback both from its users and from people who have taken our short courses indicate that many users simply find it easier to come to the information center for their occasional searches.

The public terminal, available in the information center during normal working hours, is an IBM PC/AT equipped with a Hayes Smartmodem for searching at 1200 baud and an Epson FX100 printer with a Practical Peripherals 128k microbuffer. The PC has its own IDs and passwords for the vendors to which it has access, and it uses automated logon for all searches. To facilitate the monthly billing of users for their searching, our Computing and Telecommunications Division developed a Paradox-based, online log-sheet; users must enter their names and valid charge numbers before they can begin their searches.

Brief instructions for searching options are kept next to the PC, along with a selective collection of searching aids (e.g., abbreviations used by CAS, database description sheets), lists of available databases, and price lists. Vendor help desk telephone numbers are prominently posted. Also near the PC are summary charts outlining the use of Boolean operators and truncation on STN. While the PC is in the room that houses our collection of database and vendor documentation and searching aids, etc., we have no evidence that clients ever use them. Our offices are directly across the hall, and our names and room numbers are posted on the PC.

The PC's software relevant to end-user searching includes Hayes Smartcom II, SearchMaster, and STN Express. The public terminal also offers all of the STN MENTOR tutorial programs (which are seldom used). Smartcom II provides access to the Official Airline Guide (OAG) and DIALOG Business Connection. SearchMaster provides scripts for access to ORBIT's *CA* and INSPEC databases for author and limited subject searching. STN Express provides menu (Guided Search) and command-language access to STN databases.

The availability of the public terminal and its searching options have been widely publicized. We utilize information service newsletters; multiple notices are sent to all site personnel; and signs and placards are placed throughout the laboratory and office areas as well as the information center (e.g., in the stacks near *CA* and in study carrels). We have also been successful with demonstrations given on one or more days a week, after lunch, for one to three months. In general, mailings and demonstrations seem to be most effective.

End-user searching employing SearchMaster scripts for access to ORBIT's *CA* and INSPEC databases has been available in our information center since 1985. This menu-driven approach was well received at its initiation and has been consistently used since then (see Figures 2 and 3), albeit by fewer people in recent months. Kenneth Walton, who developed the scripts, has described this SearchMaster application in detail.[6]

Briefly, the seven SearchMaster scripts available to end users provide: author searching in *CA*; reference verification (using title words and authors) in *CA*; subject searching in *CA* or INSPEC for a subject that can be defined by a single concept describable by one or two keywords; subject searching in *CA* or INSPEC for a subject that can be defined by a combination of two concepts each describable by one or two keywords; and CAS Registry number retrieval from CHEMDEX files.

In June of 1988, we added STN Express to the public terminal. For searching *CA*, its Guided Search feature provides three submenus: one for subject terms; one for document aspects (i.e., authors, document type, language, and date ranges); and one for chemical-compound aspects (i.e., names, molecular formulae, Registry Numbers, and structures). For searching databases other than *CA*, the chemical-compound aspect menus are not used and the only document aspect available is authors. Entries within any of the three submenus may be ANDed or ORed; the total contents of the three submenus may only be ANDed with each other. Truncation can be used. Thus, for example, the following strategy could be constructed:

Subject entries:

[(coal# **OR** lignite#) **AND** (liquef? **OR** gasif?)]
AND

Document-aspect entries:
[(Smith, J **AND** Jones, R) **AND** (Patent) **AND** (1970-1980)]
AND

Chemical-compound entries:
[(1234-56-7) **AND** (CO_2 **OR** CO) **AND** (1-butene)]

This ability to use a multiplicity of terms, names, and chemical aspects and to combine them is in marked contrast to our SearchMaster scripts.

When query construction is complete, Express automatically logs onto STN. In *CA* searches using chemical aspects, the Registry file is searched first, and resultant Registry Numbers are crossed over into *CA* and combined with any subject terms or document aspects. When a search is complete, the user can examine results in a trial or sample format and/or download them for printing or browsing offline. The search query is saved, and the user can modify or reuse it.

While chemical-structure input for searching the Registry file, either using Guided Search or command-language, is a major feature of STN Express, we have chosen not to equip the public terminal with a Mouse or support structure searching. Our users' research does not generally require substructure or even exact structure searching, and what structure searching is called for only infrequently benefits from structure input. We feel that structure searching requires special training: given the cost of structure searching, it is very easy to inadvertently make expensive errors.

When we loaded STN Express, we did not remove SearchMaster, even though Express's Guided Search provides for far more versatile and extensive subject and chemical compound searching than SearchMaster does. First, we felt that there were SearchMaster users who might prefer SearchMaster—and we did not want to impose a new system on users who were perfectly happy with the old one. Second, in some cases SearchMaster author searching is superior to that of Express Guided Search: Guided Search bases author searching on last name and first initial, while our SearchMaster author script can present the user with an ORBIT Neighbor list from which authors can be selected based on all forms of the name. This difference can be very useful when your author is a Jones or a Smith.

Our most recent additions to the public terminal are the Official Airline Guide (OAG) file and DIALOG Business Connection. Both were added at the request of users. Both are menu-driven, and entry to both files is carried out by Smartcom automatic logon. As of this writing we have not extensively publicized these new features, and they have not been heavily used.

ONLINE USE

While in 1988 we experienced an increase in interest in end-user searching, we need to emphasize that our population of *active* end users represents only 11% of the potential end-user population (310 individuals). If we add those who have used their IDs only once or never, our population is 18% of the research staff.

We have two quite separate groups of end users: those who use the public terminal and those with personal IDs who search on their own PCs. Those who use the public terminal do not have their own IDs, and those with IDs do not use the public terminal. Thus, it seems best to look at the two groups separately.

In 1987, there were 10 end users with their own IDs. One person had—and actively used—both an STN and a DIALOG ID. Except for one ORBIT ID holder, all 1987 ID holders searched regularly. All three ORBIT ID holders had personal copies of our SearchMaster scripts, but they ceased using ORBIT early in 1988 (Table 1).

At the end of 1988, 42 researchers had IDs, a four-fold increase over 1987. Two people hold both STN and DIALOG IDs (one used both and one used only DIALOG), and two hold both STN and ORBIT IDs (one used only STN and one did not search at all). Of these users, 19 search regularly (i.e., approximately once every two months or more), 4 searched once, and 20 have never searched. Seven of the active users consistently search several times every month; one has done so for over two years using both STN and DIALOG IDs. Five end users obtained copies of STN Express in 1988, but only one was a regular searcher.

In 1987, on average, each month, 5 people searched in 20 sessions and 4 connect hours.[9] The highest average monthly charge per person for any vendor was $13; the average monthly cost for all end-user searching was $543.

In 1988, on average, each month, 9 people searched (80% increase over 1987) in 31 sessions (55% increase) and 6 connect hours (50% increase).[9] The highest average monthly charge per person for any vendor was $11; the average monthly cost for all end-user searching was $906. Table 1 contains use data, and Figure 1 charts end-user searching for 1987 and 1988.[9]

CA is overwhelmingly the most used database, 34.60 connect

TABLE 1.
SEARCHING BY END USERS WITH PERSONAL IDs

	1987			1988		
Month	People	Sessions	Connect Hours	People	Sessions	Connect Hours
STN (1987: 4 ID Holders; 1988: 39 ID Holders)						
January	1	14	2.50	3	16	3.38
February	2	11	2.11	5	18	4.16
March	2	2	0.48	5	23	5.75
April	3	24	4.20	4	16	4.16
May	2	34	7.35	5	15	2.37
June	3	13	3.10	7	30	7.92
July	3	10	2.14	4	25	4.66
August	3	8	2.71	5	17	1.78
September	1	3	0.35	5	23	6.08
October	2	10	3.15	11	24	6.64
November	3	6	1.85	8	32	5.84
December	2	8	2.92	10	45	6.83
DIALOG (1987: 4 ID Holders; 1988: 4 ID Holders)						
January	2	15	1.19	3	16	2.27
February	2	4	0.46	3	4	0.82
March	2	3	0.29	3	4	0.50
April	2	12	1.77	4	13	1.61
May	—	—	—	4	7	0.86
June	1	4	0.54	3	5	0.69
July	4	18	2.68	1	4	0.64
August	3	7	0.72	3	3	0.41
September	2	4	0.35	2	4	0.46
October	2	3	0.57	3	16	2.24
November	1	2	0.29	2	8	0.81
December	3	3	0.59	2	6	1.43
ORBIT (1987: 3 ID Holders; 1988: 2 ID Holders)						
January	1	1	0.51	—	—	—
February	2	2	0.78	1	2	0.38
March	—	—	—	—	—	—
April	—	—	—	—	—	—
May	—	—	—	—	—	—
June	2	9	3.32	—	—	—
July	—	—	—	—	—	—
August	1	3	0.63	—	—	—
September	1	1	0.06	—	—	—
October	—	—	—	—	—	—
November	2	6	1.96	—	—	—
December	—	—	—	—	—	—

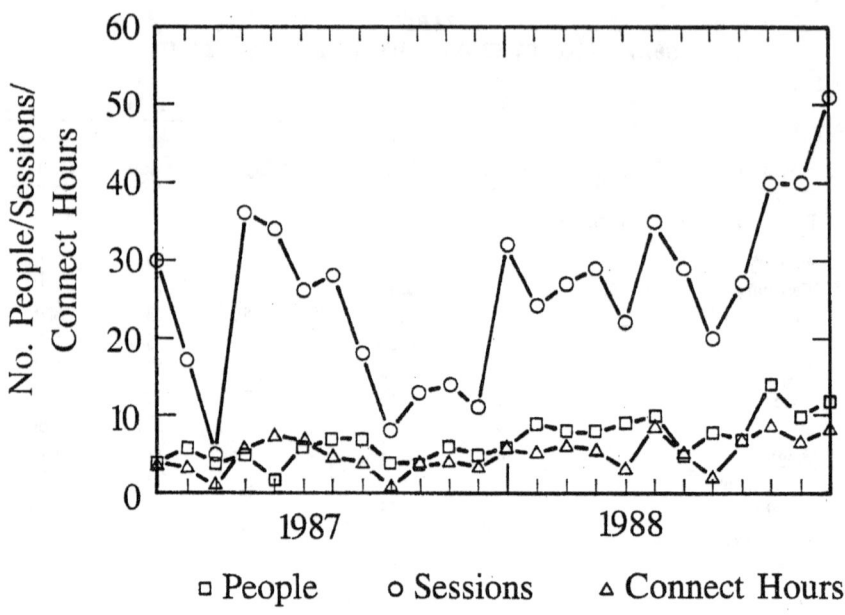

FIGURE 1. End-User Searching (1987-1988)
(End Users Searching with Personal IDs)

hours in 1987 and 36.30 connect hours in 1988. The second most used files were the *CA* Registry-related files in 1987 with 3.53 connect hours and 13C NMR in 1988 with 9.39 connect hours. Fourteen databases were used in 1987 (44.79 connect hours), while thirty were used in 1988 (65.77 connect hours). Table 2 shows database use. The actual modest use of the Registry file reinforces our decision not to support structure searching. Curiously, learning files have only been used twice in the past two years. The researchers who search 13C NMR obtained STN IDs specifically to use this file. The Official Airline Guide (OAG) was the only nontechnical database to have significant and continuing use.

With regard to public-terminal use, in 1987, on average, each month, 19 people searched in 31 sessions and 10 connect hours.[9] In 1988, on average, each month, 14 people searched (a decrease of 26% over 1987) in 24 sessions (22% decrease) and 6 connect hours (40% decrease).[9] Table 3 contains use data, and Figure 2 charts total public terminal use for 1987-1988;[9] use since June 1988 is the total

TABLE 2.
DATABASE USAGE BY END USERS WITH PERSONAL IDs

	Connect Hours	
Database (Vendor)	1987	1988
Am. Men & Women Sci. (DIALOG)	—	0.02
APILIT (STN)	—	1.41
APIPAT (STN)	—	0.27
Beilstein (STN)	—	0.05
BIOMASS (STN)	—	0.02
BIOSIS (STN)	—	0.01
C-13 NMR (STN)	—	9.39
CA (STN)	28.55	33.26
CA (DIALOG)	1.60	2.77
CA (ORBIT)	4.45	0.27
Total CA	34.60	36.30
CAOLD (STN)	—	0.06
CAPreviews (STN)	—	0.18
CASReacts (STN)	—	0.01
Chemical Eng. Abst. (DIALOG)	—	0.04
CJACS (STN)	0.12	0.79
CONF (STN)	—	0.03
CSChem (STN)	0.02	0.01
CSCorp (STN)	—	0.02
Curr. Biotech. Abst. (DIALOG)	—	0.04
DIALINDEX (DIALOG)	0.06	—
IFICDB (STN)	—	0.13
IFIPAT (STN)	—	0.16
INPADOC (STN)	—	0.06
INSPEC (STN)	—	2.39
INSPEC (DIALOG)	1.58	0.62
Total INSPEC	1.58	3.01
LRegistry (STN)	0.06	—
METADEX (DIALOG)	0.44	0.60
Moody's Corp. (DIALOG)	0.10	—
NBSThermo (STN)	—	0.08
NTIS (STN)	—	0.22
Nuclear Sci. Abst. (DIALOG)	—	0.25
OAG (DIALOG)	1.61	4.31
OnTap DIALINDEX (DIALOG)	0.04	—
Physics Briefs (STN)	0.03	3.41
Registry (STN)	2.87	2.89
CHEMNAME (DIALOG)	0.29	0.34
CHEMDEX (ORBIT)	0.37	—
Total "CA Registry Files"	3.53	3.23
SCISEARCH (DIALOG)	2.26	1.63
UFORDAT (STN)	—	0.03
World Al Abst. (DIALOG)	0.34	—
TOTAL:	44.79	65.77

TABLE 3.
SEARCHING BY END USERS AT THE PUBLIC TERMINAL

Month	1987			1988		
	People	Sessions	Connect Hours	People	Sessions	Connect Hours
January	23	33	10.00	26	33	12.01
February	23	40	13.08	18	25	7.57
March	19	36	15.87	19	30	7.93
April	19	31	10.79	17	23	6.96
May	15	23	9.43	10	16	3.90
June	23	30	9.10	7	11	2.35
July	3	27	9.43	4	5	1.67
August	18	31	8.70	1	7	1.01
September	22	38	10.97	4	8	0.92
October	22	33	9.48	4	6	1.85
November	18	29	8.98	3	5	0.96
December	21	26	7.91	2	8	1.91

of SearchMaster and STN Express use. On an average annual basis, public terminal use remains significant, but, as Figure 2 clearly shows, its use began to decline sharply in April 1988.

STN Express joined SearchMaster on the public terminal in June of 1988, and its average monthly use quickly doubled that of SearchMaster: 8 people using Express in 16 sessions and 4 connect hours; 4 people using SearchMaster in 7 sessions and 2 connect hours. Figure 3 compares SearchMaster and STN Express use beginning in June 1988.

Since SearchMaster is limited to *CA*, INSPEC, and CHEMDEX, we have not tabulated any database use statistics for it. Table 4 gives database use figures for STN Express. *CA* is again the most used, 22.16 connect hours, and INSPEC is a distant second at 0.87 connect hours.

Almost without exception, the individuals who use SearchMaster do not use STN Express, and vice versa. Curiously, STN Express users are generally not former SearchMaster users; they prove to be totally new users of the public terminal. It is also interesting that the end users who have obtained their own IDs have not generally been public terminal users. And even more fascinating, perhaps, is that the heaviest users of the information center and the professional

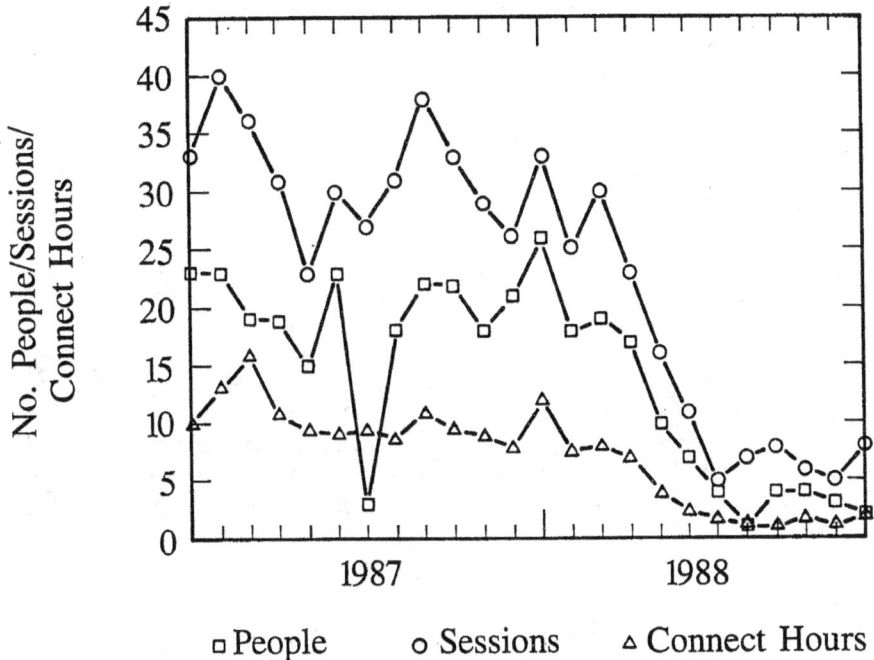

FIGURE 2. Searching Using the Public Terminal (1987-1988)

searchers' most frequent clients—two groups that are not the same—do not use the public terminal or have their own IDs.

While we have no way of knowing for certain, it is our impression that SearchMaster is currently used primarily for author searching. In 1985, when it was first introduced (and was the only public terminal option), data were collected, and 47% of its use was for author searching, 46% for subject searching, and 6% for reference verification.[6]

Because STN Express's Guided Search saves queries (so that they may be modified or reused), we were able to examine a set of 129 searches using Guided Search. Database usage was: 84% *CA*, 6% COMPENDEX, 4% INSPEC, 2% DOE Energy, 2% Registry, 1% IFIPAT, 1% METADEX, and 1% Physics Briefs. The types of searches carried out were: 40% subject searches, 19% author searches, 19% subject plus chemical-substance (i.e., using Registry

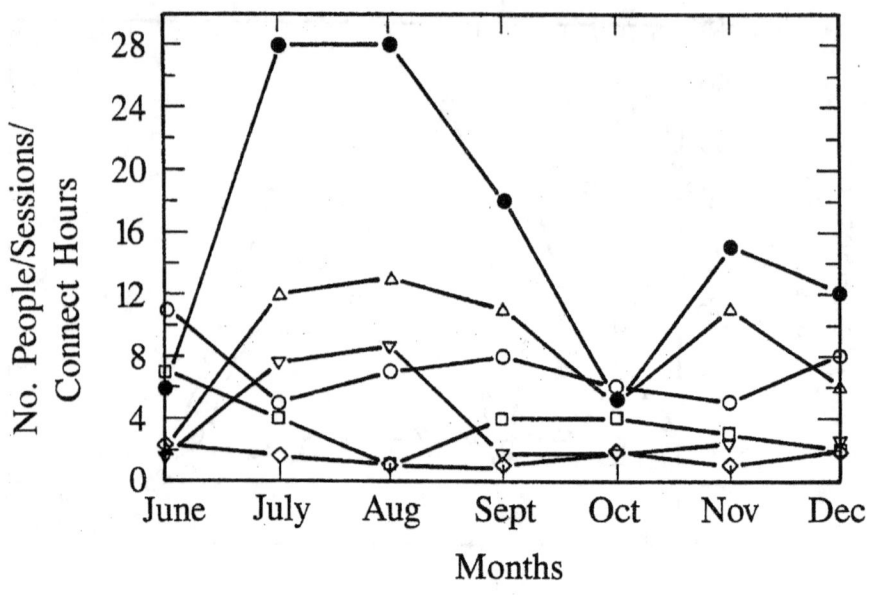

FIGURE 3. Use of SearchMaster and STN Express
(June to December 1988)

TABLE 4.
STN DATABASE USAGE
FOR STN EXPRESS ON THE PUBLIC TERMINAL
(June to December 1988)

Database	Connect Hours	Database	Connect Hours
APILIT	0.01	Energy	0.23
APIPAT	0.02	IFIPAT	0.06
BIOSIS	0.15	INSPEC	0.87
CA	22.16	Math	0.02
CAPreviews	0.08	METADEX	0.06
COMPENDEX	0.68	NTIS	0.19
CONF	0.37	Physics Briefs	0.53
DEQUIP	0.14	Registry	0.50

Numbers, molecular formulae, or compound names) searches, 12% chemical-substance searches, 8% author plus subject searches, 1% author plus chemical-substance searches, and 1% author plus subject plus chemical-substance searches. Date limitations were used in 10% of the searches, language limitations in 4%, and document type in 5%. The document-type limitations were either used to eliminate patents or to retrieve reviews and books. Language limitations were used to limit retrieval to English-language references.

CONTINUING SUPPORT

Supporting our end users has not consumed an inordinate amount of time. Once our clients have obtained their own IDs, they have been rather self-sufficient. Most calls for assistance have dealt with equipment or telecommunications problems. If their searches do fail to turn up the desired result, they tend to bring the whole search to us rather than ask for advice on strategy design. This tendency may arise from the fact that we do not offer a continuously staffed hotline; therefore, end users cannot count on reaching us when they have immediate problems. However, we cannot say how many people are calling the vendor help desks with strategy questions.

On the other hand, users of the public search terminal do call on us for advice in designing searches, as well as for help when they have equipment problems. Our immediate proximity is undoubtedly a factor, as is the fact that we personally demonstrated the system to many of these users.

We definitely perceive an opportunity for continued, pro-active assistance to our end-user population. Responses to the post-course questionnaire highlighted areas where we could approach individuals with offers of further training or personalized instruction. Time permitting, we hope to sponsor a users group for interested clients in which we shall highlight topics of general interest or bring in speakers to discuss specific databases, e.g. INSPEC or BIOSIS. Our increased visibility in this area should lead to better interactions and increasing calls for assistance.

CONCLUSIONS

Our recent experiences have shown us that end users come in many varieties: some prefer search menus, others want to use a command language; some want to search in the information center, others want to search in the comfort of their offices; some want to attend training courses, others want to read a manual and teach themselves. Still others of our clients continue to prefer to search the printed indexes, or to take all of their requests to the professional searchers.

Fears of runaway online spending by the end users or excessive demands for search consulting have proved to be unwarranted. Our clients are cost-conscious, for all are working within a budget. Our data show that they are not trying to do their own patent searching; Table 2 shows that no end user has entered the World Patents Index database in the last two years, and the entry into other patent databases seems to have been more exploration than actual use.

Each of our end-user initiatives has attracted new people and resulted in increasing numbers of searchers. Those who take courses but do not search seem glad, nevertheless, to have been exposed to training and to have the option of searching if they wish. We believe that these initiatives have increased the visibility of the searching staff and enhanced our reputation for willingness to help.

As others have found before us, many people expressing an interest in searching do not actually spend much (if any) time online. Figure 1 shows an increasing trend in the number of end-user sessions per month, but no dramatic surge. Perhaps our clients are still waiting for a perfect solution to the problem of mastering search commands, database design, and search strategies on a part-time basis. Different, partial solutions have appealed to different portions of our client population. In consultation with these clients, we shall continue our search for products, services, and teaching methods that will serve those who want to search online.

REFERENCE NOTES

1. Buntrock, Robert; Valicenti, Aldona K. End-user searching: The Amoco experience. *Journal of Chemical Information and Computer Science*. 25(4): 415-419; 1985.

2. Landsberg, M. K.; Lorenz, P. A.; Lawrence, B.; Meadows, C. T.; Hewitt,

T. T. A joint industrial-academic experiment: an evaluation of the IIDA system. *Proceedings of the American Society for Information Science (43rd Annual Meeting)*. 17: 406-408; 1980.

3. Mischo, William H.; Lee, Jounghyoun. End-user searching of bibliographic databases. *Annual Review of Information Science and Technology*. 22: 227-263; 1987.

4. Palma, Mary Ann S.; Sullivan, Charles. Meeting the needs of the end user. *Journal of Chemical Information and Computer Science*. 25(4): 422-425; 1985.

5. Reiter, Martha B. Can you teach me to do my own searching? Or tailoring online training to the needs of the end-user. *Journal of Chemical Information and Computer Science*. 25(4): 419-422; 1985.

6. Walton, Kenneth R. SearchMaster—programmed for the end-user. *Online (Weston, Connecticut)*. 10(5): 70-79; 1986.

7. Walton, K. R.; Dedert, P. L. Experiences at Exxon in training end users to search technical databases online. *Online (Weston, Connecticut)*. 7(5): 42-50; 1983.

8. Warr, Wendy A.; Haygarth Jackson, Angela R. End-user searching of CAS ONLINE. Results of a cooperative experiment between Imperial Chemical Industries and Chemical Abstracts Service. *Journal of Chemical Information and Computer Science*. 28(2): 72-78; 1988.

9. With regard to the statistics we have used, a "person" is counted only once each month—the first time that an individual searches in any month. A "session" is bounded by a logon, a logoff and a reasonable period of time; a logoff immediately followed by a logon is not counted as a new session. A session may comprise the use of multiple databases and the same database may be used multiple times. "Connect hours" include those for substantive database use and associated time in the "Home" file. Instances in which the user logs into the Home file and logs out without entering a substantive database are not counted: this is not considered a session; the user is not counted as a person; and connect hours are not tabulated.

The Role of Medical Libraries in End-User Searching: Teaching the MEDLINE Database to Health Care Professionals

Beryl Glitz

SUMMARY. End-user searching is extremely popular in the health care community because of urgent need for access to the lastest biomedical information and the ability of a single database, MEDLINE, to provide much of this information. Medical libraries have taken a proactive role in training health care professionals to search MEDLINE in its various guises. The complexity of the database and the number of different access systems have led to a variety of classes and a strong commitment on the part of medical libraries to act as educational and consultative agents in the area of biomedical end-user searching.

INTRODUCTION

The health care community has been an ardent user of online literature search services since the early seventies when the National Library of Medicine (NLM) released its Medical Literature Analysis and Retrieval System (MEDLARS) for interactive searching.[1] Because of the rapid developments which are continually taking place in medical research and the increasingly higher expectations and demand for improved patient care, the information needs of health care professionals are frequent, often urgent and almost

---

Beryl Glitz is Educational Services Coordinator in the Reference Division of the Louise Darling Biomedical Library, UCLA, Center for the Health Sciences, 10833 Le Conte Avenue, Los Angeles, CA 90024-1798. She received her MLS degree from the UCLA Graduate School of Library and Information Science.

always for the latest knowledge. Ready access to relevant current citations in the biomedical literature via the computer, has clearly been a boon to this community.

It is no suprise then, that with the advent of end-user searching, the health care field was foremost in the demand for this type of self-service. While other fields have clearly benefitted from online literature retrieval and the move to end-user searching, what is unique to the medical area and an important factor behind the rapid developments in this area, is the ability of a single bibliographic database, MEDLINE, to answer an enormous percentage of information requests.

THE STRUCTURE OF MEDLINE

The MEDLINE database, developed first as a means for more rapidly producing *Index Medicus*, the major printed index to medical periodical literature, now provides online access to the references in some 3,400 journals from all over the world. With its millions of records, organized into chronological files, MEDLINE has been likened to an "idealized medical record department" where each record represents a separate journal article with specific pieces of information (e.g. author's name, title words) arranged within the record for easy retrieval.[2] Beyond this bibliographic information, however, each record includes specific subject headings which describe the contents of the article. The use of these standardized Medical Subject Headings, MeSH headings as they are commonly known, by the specialists who index the articles added to the database, is what separates MEDLINE from many other bibliographic databases. While most other databases provide subject access only through the actual terms used by authors in their titles and abstracts, MeSH headings provide a consistent and precise method of subject retrieval. Moreover, the use of standardized sub-headings, attached to the MeSH headings, which describe commonly occurring aspects of health care such as diagnosis, drug therapy, and the like, allow the searcher to more narrowly specify the type of article sought. As well as specificity in searching, the grouping of MeSH headings into hierarchical "trees" of related terms and the ability to "explode" these trees so as to easily capture all articles indexed with related headings, greatly improves the recall in any MEDLINE search. This paper will look at the role of medical libraries in training both students and professionals in the health care field in searching this sophisticated database in all its various guises.

MULTIPLE ACCESS TO MEDLINE

While the features described above provide enormous power in subject searching in MEDLINE, they can also act as a stumbling block to the searcher. Without a clear understanding of the application of MeSH, the use of subheadings and the place of exploding in a search, relevant citations can easily be missed.[3] When MEDLINE searches were almost all performed by trained intermediaries, using the rather complex MEDLARS native command language, ELHILL, the complexity of the database was not seen as a barrier to search retrieval. However, with the advent of end-user searching, the different vendors of MEDLINE have had to develop various methods to cope with the complexities of the database and to provide a more user-friendly environment. Apart from the original access through the National Library of Medicine and its ELHILL search language, the large commercial vendors like BRS and Dialog, have provided access to MEDLINE for many years, first through their own full-search systems and later through more user-friendly services such as BRS-Colleague and Knowledge Index. In the last decade, individual institutions have provided several different systems for accessing either all or part of MEDLINE, starting in 1979 with PaperChase from Beth Israel Hospital in Boston which was developed as a menu-driven system.[4] Mini Medline was introduced at the Georgetown University Medical Center in 1982,[5] and more recently, MELVYL MEDLINE was developed at the University of California with both a menu- and a command-driven search capability.[6] In 1986, the National Library of Medicine brought out its own user-friendly method for searching MEDLINE, a disk-based package for use with IBM-compatible personal computers called GRATEFUL MED,[7] and in the same year, another pc-based package, Med-Base was introduced by Online Research Systems, Inc.[8] With the advent of CD-ROM technology, new versions of MEDLINE quickly became available from a number of companies, starting with Compact Cambridge MEDLINE from Cambridge Scientific.[9] A recent article in *Database* lists seventeen different methods of accessing the database online, and eight CD-ROM versions.[10]

The Commercial Vendors' Role in Training

In spite of the variety of vendors and versions, the underlying database, MEDLINE, has retained its same basic structure and use of MeSH terminology. Thus, in providing access to MEDLINE for the end user, the different vendors have had to cope in more or less successful ways with the problems of providing a user-friendly interface while maintaining the detailed retrieval capabilities of the database. Although billed as user-friendly, the various commercial end-user search systems usually require at least some type of initial training, especially for the many health professionals completely new to online searching. Vendors generally provide some initial instruction to the end users who buy into their systems, while toll-free help numbers and manuals are other popular sources of assistance. It has not been cost-effective, however, for these companies to mount any type of large-scale educational programs. Recently, vendors such as Dialog have provided training videos to assist people in searching, but it has been left largely to the medical library community to provide widespread and consistant training, in a variety of ways to the growing number of end users in the health care community.

The Role of The National Library of Medicine in Training

In this area of online search training, medical libraries have had an able leader and supporter in the National Library of Medicine. Acknowledging the complexity of its databases and the MeSH system, NLM has been committed to training searchers since the seventies when it first provided three-week-long classes, primarily for librarians. Through the online training component of its Regional Medical Library (RML) network, NLM has been able to train hundreds of people all over the country to search MEDLINE and its various other databases. Classes have always been of high quality and provide in-depth information on indexing policies and search strategy. In response to the demand for end-user training, NLM has shortened this basic course to encourage health-professionals to attend, and has also developed a model course entitled "The Basics of Searching MEDLINE" for libraries to use and/or adapt for their own in-house training in the ELHILL search system; the course comes complete with a detailed manual and syllabus. Along with the course, NLM also offers a workshop entitled "Teaching Health Professionals the Basics of Searching MEDLINE" which covers basic teaching techniques and a variety of other helpful suggestions to assist medical librarians in teaching MEDLINE to health professionals.

The Role of Medical Libraries in Training

From this basic course and the tremendous amount of practical assistance provided by the workshop, medical libraries developed training programs for their particular clientele. But because of the many ways to access MEDLINE, libraries have moved beyond the Basics type of class with its use of ELHILL for searching, and have developed a variety of courses to teach the different search systems and explain the intricacies of the database. A recent survey of 121 medical school libraries in the United States showed that 78 of the 113 responding libraries have some type of end-user program; mostly formal classes.[11] Several types of systems are being taught, including BRS/Colleague, BRS/AfterDark, Knowledge Index, and PaperChase, though MEDLINE through NLM was the overwhelmingly popular system (68%). While the goal of all these classes is to familiarize health professionals with the particular system peculiarities, most classes typically spend some time going over MEDLINE and introducing the concept of MeSH headings. Indeed, a whole course devoted just to MeSH is taught by some institutions to appeal to the various system searchers.[12]

Medical libraries can therefore be seen as filling the gap between the various MEDLINE search systems and the health care end user who traditionally has had little or no previous online searching experience. While commercial vendors provide some training tools, they are, quite naturally, more concerned with selling their products, and rely on the librarians to be the educational agents for database searching. And although NLM continues to maintain the database and provide training support, it is the practicing medical librarians who best understand the ways their patrons use and look for information and who are therefore best situated to provide impartial advice and knowledgable training for end users.

END-USER CLASSES

A typical end-user training class must cover many topics beyond the actual search mechanics. Class attendees must deal with the problems of dividing a search into component parts, translating those components into appropriate headings and/or text words, and using Boolean operators to address the problems of precision and recall. The proper use of MeSH is a major part of the syllabus, including access to the headings from the various printed lists, manipulation of the trees, the use of subheadings and check tags, explosions and truncation. Most classes will also include some hands-on time to reinforce what has been taught.

Apart from the intellectual content of the class, a host of other factors need to be dealt with. First and foremost is the nature of the class participants: usually those who come are adult learners, often with little knowledge or downright fear of computers, and always busy: fitting any class into the hectic schedule of a health care practitioner is a challenge all by itself. To this must be added the problems of advertising the class, setting up terminals, arranging for passwords to use during class and often, deciding on an appropriate fee to charge, since many institutions do not have any budget to support the costs of end-user training. Some libraries even secure continuing education credit for their classes to make them more appealing to physicians.

END-USER TRAINING FOR STUDENTS

While the first end-user classes were largely aimed at the practicing physician and medical researcher, now that such training is firmly established, medical libraries have recently turned their attention to the various groups of students in the health care field. A recent survey was conducted by the Association of Academic

Health Science Library Directors to discover the extent of online search training being offered to students by its member libraries.[13] Preliminary results show that 85% of the respondants (81 libraries) are providing some type of training; 99% training medical students, 62% nursing students and 75% graduate biomedical sciences students. Almost all of the libraries (98%) teach MEDLINE from a variety of vendors, including CD-ROM versions; 62% are using the GRATEFUL MED software. Though a relatively new phenomenon, some medical schools are actually beginning to require online search training as part of the curriculum, a trend fostered by the 1986 GPEP report which strongly recommended this skill as necessary for the physician of the future.[14]

The Future of End-User Training

In describing the variety and extent of classes being offered, it is clear that the medical library community has taken a strong, proactive role in end-user training. With the growing numbers of personal computers in offices, schools and clinics, the continued need for rapid access to the latest biomedical information, and a mandate for teaching future health care professionals, medical libraries will certainly continue in this role for the forseeable future. With the suppport of NLM, libraries are deeply committed to providing their expertise as teachers and consultants in online literature searching and developing new courses, new methods of teaching as search systems continue to change and multiply. Moreover, with the knowledge that "in medicine, where the care of a patient may be influenced by the results of the search"[15] medical libraries are also taking an active part in testing new search systems and working with manufacturers to ensure the quality and usefulness of these products.[16] This new role, in partnership with commercial vendors, is just one more step in the continuing tradition of medical library service to the nation's health care community.

REFERENCES

1. Mehnert, Robert B.; Leiter, Joseph. The National Library of Medicine. *In*: Darling, Louise, ed. *Handbook of medical librarianship Vol. III. Health science librarianship and administration.* Chicago : Medical Library Association; 1988; p. 143-176.

2. Bickers, Rex G. Online medical information services. *Primary Care*. 12(3): 459-482; 1985 September.

3. Sewell, Winifred; Teitelbaum, Sandra. Observations of end-user online searching behavior over eleven years. *Journal of the American Society for Information Science*. 37(4): 234-245; 1986 July.

4. Horowitz, Gary L.; Bleich, Howard L. PaperChase: a computer program to search the medical literature. *New England Journal of Medicine*. 305: 924-930; 1981 October.

5. Broering, Naomi C. The Mini MEDLINE system: a library-based end-user search system. *Bulletin of the Medical Library Association*. 73(2): 138-145; 1985 April.

6. Renford, Beverly. Searching MELVYL MEDLINE. *DLA Bulletin*. 8(3): 1, 3-7; 1988 Fall.

7. Snow, Bonnie; Corbett, Ann L.; Brahmi, Frances A. GRATEFUL MED: NLM's front end software. *Database*. 9(6): 94-99; 1986 December.

8. Snow, Bonnie. Med-Base: ease of use and search accuracy. *Online*. 11(3): 125-133; 1987 May.

9. Capodagli, James A.; Mardikian, Jackie; Uva, Peter A. MEDLINE on compact disc: end-user searching on Compact Cambridge. *Bulletin of the Medical Library Association*. 76(2): 181-183; 1988 April.

10. Van Camp, Ann J. The many faces of MEDLINE. *Database*. 11(5): 101-107; 1988 October.

11. Welborn, Victoria; Kuehn, Jennifer J. End-user programs in medical school libraries: a survey. *Bulletin of the Medical Library Association*. 76(2): 137-140; 1988 April.

12. For example, "Subject Searching in the MEDLINE Database" taught by the Louise Darling Biomedical Library, University of California, Los Angeles and "MeSH and Textword Searching" taught by the Norris Medical Library, University of Southern California.

13. Association of Academic Health Sciences Library Directors. *Online search training by academic health sciences libraries*. 1988. Unpublished Survey.

14. Muller, Steven. (Chairman). Physicians for the Twenty-First Century. Report of the Project Panel on the General Professional Education of the Physician and College Preparation for Medicine. *Journal of Medical Education*. 59(part 2): 1-200; 1984 November.

15. Miller, Naomi; Kirby, Martha; Templeton, Etheldra. MEDLINE on CD-ROM: end user searching in a medical school library. *Medical Reference Services Quarterly*. 7(3): 1-13; 1988.

16. Glitz, Beryl. Testing the new technology: MEDLINE on CD-ROM in an academic health science library. *Special Libraries*. 79(1): 28-33; 1988 Winter.

A *Chemical Abstracts* Training Seminar for Science Librarians

Bruce Slutsky

SUMMARY. Science librarians at the New York Public Library without a strong educational background in chemistry often had difficulty in searching the printed *Chemical Abstracts*. A one-hour seminar was held to teach the fundamentals of *Chemical Abstracts* with an emphasis on finding references to well known chemical substances. Uses of the Index Guide, Author Index, General Subject Index, Chemical Substance Index, Chemical Formula Index, Patent Index, and Index of Ring Systems were shown. A brief discussion of online searching of *Chemical Abstracts* followed. Participants were given a set of exercises and a reading list of guides to the chemical literature.

The Science and Technology Research Center of the New York Public Library provides reference service in a wide range of disciplines in the physical sciences and applied technologies. A significant number of patrons request information about chemical products. The reference librarians, except for the author, do not have strong educational backgrounds in science. On several occasions they had difficulty answering chemistry reference questions. The aim of this seminar was to teach the fundamentals of searching the printed *Chemical Abstracts* to science librarians. Emphasis was placed on searching for known chemical products. Other sources such as the *Merck Index, Kirk-Othmer Encyclopedia of Chemical Technology*, the *Applied Science and Technology Index, Science*

Bruce Slutsky is Coordinator of Online Services for the New York Public Library, Science and Technology Research Center, 5th Ave. at 42nd St., New York, NY 10018. He received the BS (Chemistry) at City College of New York, MS (Chemistry) at University of Rhode Island, and MS (Information Science) at Pratt Institute. He previously worked as a chemist in the pharmaceutical and flavor and fragrances industries.

© 1990 by The Haworth Press, Inc. All rights reserved.

Citation Index, and the *Dictionary of Organic Compounds* were discussed briefly. A secondary goal was to show how these sources can be used in conjunction with the printed *Chemical Abstracts*. A short discussion of online searching of the DIALOG Chemical Substance Files and the *Chemical Abstracts* bibliographic files followed.

The training session was organized as follows:

  I. Coverage and Organization of *Chemical Abstracts*
 II. Use of Indexes
    A. Author Index
    B. General Subject Index
    C. Chemical Substance Index
    D. Chemical Formula Index
    E. Patent Index
    F. Index of Ring Systems
III. Online Searching of *Chemical Abstracts*
    A. DIALOG Chemical Substance Files
    B. *Chemical Abstracts* files on DIALOG

Exercises were provided to give the trainees experience in using the indexes as they were introduced. A set of exercises at the end of the session was given to test the trainees' ability to use a variety of chemical literature sources. Many of these exercises were questions that were posed to reference librarians. A reading list of sources in the Science and Technology Research Center was provided.

I. COVERAGE AND ORGANIZATION OF CHEMICAL ABSTRACTS

Document Types Covered

1. Journal articles—including review articles.
2. Congresses and symposia proceedings.
3. Technical reports.
4. Deposited documents.
5. Dissertations.
6. New books and audio-visual materials.
7. Patents.

Nature of the Abstracts

They are not to be evaluative or critical. Their goal is to give the researcher quick access to the chemical content of the document sufficient to determine if the original document should be consulted. The abstracts include:

1. The purpose and scope of the reported work.
2. New reactions, substances, techniques, procedures, apparatus, and properties.
3. New applications.
4. Results of the investigations with the author's interpretations and conclusions.

Chemical Abstracts is published weekly. The odd numbered issues contain:

    20 Biochemistry sections
    14 Organic Chemistry sections

The even numbered issues contain:

    12 Macromolecular Chemistry sections (Polymer Science)
    18 Applied Chemistry and Chemical Engineering sections
    16 Physical, Inorganic, and Analytical Chemistry sections
    80 sections in total.

Each issue includes a Keyword index, Patent index, and Author index for current awareness searching.

When is *Chemical Abstracts* not the appropriate source?

1. Business and company information.
2. Statistics.
3. For articles in general science magazines.
4. Clinical medicine — Some animal and in vitro studies are covered in the biochemistry sections.
5. Basic information that can be found in a textbook.
6. Physical Constants of common compounds (boiling point, melting point, density, solubility, etc.).

EXERCISE 1

Take 10 or 15 minutes to browse through 2 consecutive issues of *Chemical Abstracts* to see the vastness of the discipline of chemistry. Observe how it overlaps and interacts with the other physical and life sciences.

II. USE OF INDEXES

A. Author Index
B. General Subject Index
C. Chemical Substance Index
D. Chemical Formula Index
E. Patent Index
F. Index of Ring Systems

A. Author Index

1. Only the first author of a paper is directly searchable. *See* references are given for coauthors.
2. A corporate author will be given only for patents. A "P" in front of an abstract number indicates the document is a patent. Thus in *CA* you can search for chemical patents of a given company. If you are looking for journal papers published by scientists from a particular company or university you must search the Source Index of Science Citation Index. Such information may be found online by using the prefixed field CS= (Corporate Source).

EXERCISE 2

There is one paper in *CA* written by Bruce Slutsky. Find it.

EXERCISE 3

Find a patent by Hoffmann-LaRoche on dehydroxypantolactone 1985 or later.

B. General Subject Index

As you can see in Table 1, the General Subject Index (GSI) was not a separate entity until the 9th Collective Index. Before that time chemical substances and subjects were combined into the Subject Index. The following subjects are covered (examples are taken from the index for Volume 105):

1. Classes of chemical substances — Alcohols
2. Subject terms — Boilers
3. Physical and chemical phenomena — Crosslinking
4. Reactions — Cannizzaro Reaction
5. Chemical Technology — Heat-resistant materials

TABLE 1

Collective Index	1.	2.	3.	4.	5.	6.	7.	8.	9.	10.	11.
Years covered	1907-16	1917-26	1927-36	1937-46	1947-56	1957-61	1962-66	1967-71	1972-76	1977-81	1982-86
CA Volumes	1-10	11-20	21-30	31-40	41-50	51-55	56-65	66-75	76-85	86-95	96-105
Index Guide									X	X	X	X
Gen. Subject Index									X	X	X
Chem. Substance Index									X	X	X
Subject Index	X	X	X	X	X	X	X	X			
Formula Index		27-Year Collective Formula Index (1920-1946)			X	X	X	X	X	X	X
Index of Ring System		(contained in the introduction to the Subject Index)					X	X	X	X	X
Author Index	X	X	X	X	X	X	X	X	X	X	X
Patent Index										X	X
Numerical Patent Index				10-Year Num. P.I	X	X	X	X	X		
Patent Concordance							X	X	X		

This table was reproduced with permission, VCH Publishers, Inc., from Schulz, Hedda, *From CA to CAS Online*. New York: VCH; 1988. 227p.

6. Industrial processes and equipment — Carbonization and Coking (process) and Converters (equipment)
7. Scientific designations for animals, plants, and microorganisms — Fungi
8. Biological and medical terminology — Genes and Genetic Element

Various qualifiers:

1. Analysis
2. Biological Studies
3. Occurrence
4. Preparation
5. Properties
6. Reactions
7. Uses

INDEX GUIDE!!

Before any searching is attempted, the Index Guide should be consulted. It provides cross-references to the various *CA* volume indexes. It is not an index referring to the abstract numbers. It comprises an alphabetical ordered collection of subject terms, synonyms, acronyms, trivial and trade names, and all concepts which are not used in the strictly controlled vocabulary of the indexes. There are no index guides prior to the 8th Collective Index (1967-71). For those periods *see* and *see also* references appear in the Subject Index. Examples from the 10th Collective Index Guide:

Apertives — see cathartics

Antisepsis — see Bactericidal action and bacteriostatic action or sterilization and disinfection.

Polyols — see Alcohols, polyhydric

An R appearing before the entry indicates that it is a review article which summarizes research done by others. A B before the entry indicates that it is a book.

For the following three exercises use only Volume 104 covering January-June 1986:

EXERCISE 4

Find a reference to optical absorption by chromium oxide coatings.

EXERCISE 5

Find a review article on the uses of platinum to inhibit the growth of cancer.

EXERCISE 6

Find a patent for antioxidants in cosmetics.

C. Chemical Substance Index

Before we can discuss how to search for substances in *CA*, it would be useful to familiarize ourselves with the different types of substances.

1. Elements—An element is defined as a kind of matter that contains only one type of atom. The elements are shown in the Periodic Table of the Elements which can be found in any chemistry textbook.
2. Compounds—When two or more different elements combine chemically to make a new substance it is called a compound. Types of compounds:
   a. Inorganic substances—obtained in one way or another from the earth. Many inorganic substances are synthesized in the laboratory. They usually consist of a metal (left side of the Periodic Table) and a non-metal (right side of the Periodic Table).
   b. Organic substances—Chemists in the early 19th century believed that organic compounds could only be obtained from animal or plant sources. It was later determined that these compounds could be synthesized in the laboratory. Organic substances have at least one carbon atom.
   c. Organometallic compounds include compounds of elements that possess metal-like properties and that are chemically combined with one or more carbon atoms Tetraethyl lead, a gasoline additive, is an example.

d. A polymer or macromolecule is a high molecular weight material of either synthetic or natural origin. There is usually a repeating unit. Polyethylene, polystyrene, and polyvinylchloride are examples.
e. Alloy — a metal product containing two or more elements as a solid solution, as an intermetallic compound or as a mixture of metallic phases.
f. Biomolecules — chemicals from living systems. Examples are enzymes, proteins, nucleic acids, peptides, amino acids, and lipids.

Literature Searching for Specific Chemical Compounds

A research chemist plans a synthesis with a target molecule in mind. He will plan a synthesis to start with commercially available materials. Usually there are several steps involved before the target molecule can be obtained.

```
A -------------> B ----------> C ---------------> D -----------> E
Commercially
available              ------------>intermediates ------------> Final Product
chemical(s)
```

Before he/she even starts an experiment in the laboratory, a chemist must determine if this chemical entity he proposes as new has been ever reported in the journal or patent literature. Literally months of laboratory work can be wasted if such a literature search is not done. If the desired final product has never been reported, the chemist may want to know if any of the intermediates have been previously synthesized. It is not necessary to rediscover the wheel.

Almost all of the researchers of the STC chemistry collection are searching for substances that are already known. Chemical substances very often have several names either commercial or nonproprietary.

For example, nitroglycerin, which is used as an explosive and as a drug for angina, has the following names as reported in the *Merck Index*: glyceryl trinitrate, trinitroglycerol, glonin, trinitrin, Nirolid,

Nitrodisc, and many more. Rather than clutter the Chemical Substance Index with numerous *see* references, the Index Guide was published to show the approved *CA* name. This *CA* name is based on the structure of the molecule. The *CA* name for nitroglycerin for the 9th Collective Index and later is 1,2,3, propanetriol, trinitrate. Any searching in *CA* from 1972 onward for this substance will have to be done under this name. At this point I must introduce the concept of registry numbers (RN). The RN is the "Social Security Number" of a specific chemical substance. Every substance entered in *CA* from the 8th Collective Index (1967-71) onward is assigned a registry number. For nitroglycerin it is 53-63-0. Thus a registry number rather than a substance name must be used to search *CA* in an online system. The registry number contains no inherent information about the chemical composition or structure of the substance. These numbers are now cited in many journals, handbooks, and reference sources listing chemicals. Chemical manufacturers are required to use them in accordance with new laws governing chemicals. CAS has a Registry Handbook Number section. It lists the registry numbers in sequence, followed by the *CA* systematic name and the molecular formula. After that, the Chemname, Chemsis files on DIALOG (to be discussed later) can be used to determine the *CA* name for a known registry number.

To confuse you even further, I must tell you that *CA* names of substances change as one searches the earlier collective indexes. A major change in the naming of substances occurred for the 9th Collective Index (1972-76) and later. For example, Nitroglycerin is the *CA* name for Nitroglycerin in the 8th Collective Index. Even if the *CA* name changes from the 8th to the 9th Collective Index, the registry number remains the same.

EXERCISE 7

Find the registry number for aspirin. Determine its name for the 8th, 9th and 10th Collective periods using the respective Index Guide. Try to find it in the 7th Collective Index. Remember, there is no Index Guide for this period, but *see* references are given in the General Subject Index.

EXERCISE 8

Toluene is a common organic chemical used as a solvent. Find references to it in all collective indexes of *CA*.

D. Chemical Formula Index

All substances mentioned in a particular *CA* volume are listed in the Formula Index. There can be many different substances with the same chemical formula.

EXERCISE 9

Check any formula index for $C_7H_7NO_3$ to see how many different substances there are with this formula.
Each molecular formula is followed by the various systematic *CA* Index names, the appropriate *CA* registry numbers, and the corresponding abstracts. If numerous citations are given for one substance name, a cross-reference to the Chemical Substance Index is given. A disadvantage of the Chemical Formula Index is that no text modifications to the original abstracts is provided. Thus the Chemical Substance Index should be consulted once the *CA* Index name has been determined. This index is useful when a searcher knows the chemical formula but is not certain of the *CA* nomenclature.

E. Patent Index

The Patent Index contains information on patent documents processed by CAS during the current volume. It replaces the *CA* Numerical Patent Index and the *CA* Patent Concordance (see chart). The Patent Index includes entries for all newly abstracted patents which document an invention and cross-references to the first abstracted document on an invention when more than one document describes that invention.
As an example, we'll look at the Patent Index for Volume 102. The countries are listed at the beginning.

Examples:
US Patent 4,474,970 see *CA* reference 102:62,249w
US Patent 4,477,606 see EP (European Patent Organization) 106363 A2 which is *CA* reference 101:92608j

EXERCISE 10

Using Index Volume 105, find a United States Patent by Pfizer for a Prazosin-pirbuterol combination for bronchodilation. There are two ways that this patent can be found.

F. Index of Ring Systems

Organic compounds exist as straight chains or rings. A very simple example of a ring compound is benzene. An example of a fused ring system is naphthalene. All atoms on the ring are carbon. When a ring contains more than one kind of atom, it is known as a heterocycle. Pyridine is an example.

Substituent groups can be added to different positions on the rings. The nomenclature of these compounds are dependent on the rings and the placement of the substituents.

The Index of Ring Systems lists the names of the cyclic skeletons contained in organic chemical compounds in the order determined by their ring analyses.

This index should be used only by searchers with knowledge of chemistry. Please be aware of its role in the determination of chemical nomenclature.

III. ONLINE SEARCHING OF CHEMICAL ABSTRACTS

Chemical Abstracts is searchable through DIALOG and STN International among other vendors. On DIALOG, only the bibliographic information and index terms are searchable and displayable. Abstracts may be searched and displayed on STN International. The search mechanics for STN are somewhat different than those of DIALOG. Training materials and a learning diskette are available for those interested in learning to use this system.

A. DIALOG Chemical Substance Files

Files 300, 301, 328, 329, 330, 331, 332.

These are nonbibliographic files of chemical substances registered through CAS since 1967. They contain the CAS registry number, molecular formula, CAS substance name(s), synonyms, ring data and other chemical substance information. Table 2 summarizes the files.

Files 328-332 include substances that are cited only *once* in the literature.

File 300 includes substances in the CAS Registry system which have not been cited in the literature since 1967.

Chemname (File 301) includes those chemical substances in the CAS Registry System that have been referenced two or more times from 1967 to the present.

Patrons of the New York Public Library Science and Technology Division are generally interested in known chemical products which would be found only in file 301. About 75-80% of all chemical substances have been cited only once in the literature.

These files can be searched if one knows a registry number and needs to find its *CA* name or if one has a common name and needs to know its *CA* name(s) or registry numbers. Here are two examples:

B 301

? s calcium(w)benzoate

```
              4054     CALCIUM
             12674     BENZOATE

      S1        1      CALCIUM(W)BENZOATE
```
? t 1/5/1

1/5/1

   CAS REGISTRY NUMBER: 2090-05-3
   FORMULA: C7H602.1/2Ca
   RING SYSTEM DATA:

TABLE 2. DIALOG File Data

File	File No.	Collective Index Period	Inclusive Dates	Update Frequency	File Size
CHEMZERO	300		1965–	as available	1,545,826
CHEMNAME	301		1967–	quarterly	1,959,227
CHEMSIS	328	8th	1967–1971	irregular	803,884
	329	9th	1972–1976	irregular	1,090,665
	330	10th	1977–1981	irregular	1,288,792
	331	11th	1982–1986	irregular	1,400,073
	332	12th	1987–	quarterly	247,005

(01) (nr=01; sr=6; ar= fr=C6.01; ir=46-150-18)
CA NAME(S):
HP=Benzoic acid (8CI 9CI), NM=calcium salt
HP=Calcium benzoate
SYNONYMS: Calcium dibenzoate; Benzocalol;

? s rn=104088-79-1

      S3   1   RN=104088-79-1

? t 3/5/1

3/5/1

CAS REGISTRY NUMBER: 104088-79-1
FORMULA: C28H22F2N2O
RING SYSTEM DATA:
(01) (nr=01; sr=6; ar= fr=C6.01; ir=46-150-18)
(01) (nr=05; sr=5,6,6,6,6; ar=C4N.01-C4NO.01-C6.03; fr=NC4.01-NC2OC2.01-C6.03; ir=8161-5-1)
CA NAME(S):
HP=Spiro(2H-indole-2,3'-(3H)naphth(2,1-b)(1,4)oxazine) (9CI), SB= 1-((2,4-difluorophenyl)methyl)-1,3-dihydro-3,3-dimethyl-

B. Chemical Abstracts *Files on DIALOG*

File 399 – CA from 1967-Present
File 308 – 8th CI 1967-71
File 309 – 9th CI 1972-76
File 310 – 10th CI 1977-81
File 311 – 11th CI 1982-86
File 312 – 12th CI 1987-Present

It would take a few hours to discuss in detail online searching in *CA*. Here are a few hints.

1. Always use registry numbers for searching chemical substances.
2. Use the L or S operators to decrease the possibility of obtaining false drops.
3. To limit a search to patents – ss s1/pat

4. To limit a search to nonpatents—ss s1/npt
5. In a search strategy use both the approved *CA* abbreviation and the full term.
6. Use PA= for Patent Assignee. Use the expand command.
7. Use CS= for corporate source. This covers both patents and journals to give the affiliation of the author(s).

Here is a search for Valium or Diazepam RN=439-14-5 which illustrates some of the points mentioned above.

File 399:CA SEARCH 1967-1988 UD=10908

(Copr. 1988 by the Amer. Chem. Soc.)

Set	Items	Description

? s rn=439-14-5

    S1   6390   RN=439-14-5

? ss s1(1)(detn or determination)
Processing
Processing
Processing
Processing
Processing
Processing

Set	Items	Description
S2	6390	S1/DE
S3	514573	DETN/DE (DETERMINATION)
S4	5216	DETERMINATION/DE
S5	531	S1(L)(DETN OR DETERMINATION)

? t 5/3/1-5

5/3/1

    109031454 CA: 109(5)31454z JOURNAL
    Use of micellar mobile phases and microbore column switching for the assay of drugs in physiological fluids
    AUTHOR(S): Koenigbauer, Michael J.; Curtis, Michael A.

LOCATION: ICI Pharm. Group, ICI Americas Inc., Wilmington, DE, 19897, USA
JOURNAL: J. Chromatogr. DATE: 1988 VOLUME: 427 NUMBER: 2 PAGES: 277-85 CODEN: JOCRAM ISSN: 0021-9673 LANGUAGE: English

5/3/2

109027668 CA: 109(4)27668e JOURNAL
Polarographic reduction of sulazepam (a sulfur analog of diazepam) and its possible analytical use
AUTHOR(S): Weber, J. M.; Volke, J.
LOCATION: Ustav Fyz. Chem. Elektrochem. J. Heyrovskeho, CSAV, Prague, Czech.
JOURNAL: Cesk. Farm. DATE: 1988 VOLUME: 37 NUMBER: 3 PAGES: 97-103 CODEN: CKFRAY ISSN: 0009-0530 LANGUAGE: Czech

5/3/3

109000935 CA: 109(1)935c JOURNAL
Results for 74 substances tested for interference with determination of plasma catecholamines by "high-performance" liquid chromatography with electrochemical detection
AUTHOR(S): Koller, Marianne
LOCATION: Recipe Pharma Vertriebs G.m.b.H. and Co., D-8000/60, Munich, Fed. Rep. Ger.
JOURNAL: Clin. Chem. (Winston-Salem, N.C.) DATE: 1988 VOLUME: 34 NUMBER: 5 PAGES: 947-9 CODEN: CLCHAU ISSN: 0009-9147 LANGUAGE: English

5/3/4

108226969 CA: 108(26)226969h JOURNAL
Totally automated robotic system for liquid chromatographic analysis of solid dosage formulations with the aid of a reduced Kalman filter
AUTHOR(S): Matsuda, Rieko; Hayashi, Yuzuru; Ishibashi, Mumio; Takeda, Yasushi
LOCATION: Div. Drugs, Natl. Inst. Hyg. Sci., Tokyo, Japan,

JOURNAL: J. Chromatogr. DATE: 1988 VOLUME: 438 NUMBER: 2 PAGES: 319-27 CODEN: JOCRAM ISSN: 0021-9673 LANGUAGE: English

5/3/5

108215730 CA: 108(25)215730x JOURNAL
Simultaneous determination of quinidine and hydroquinidine in the presence of benzodiazepines in human plasma
AUTHOR(S): Quaglio, M. P.; Bellini, A. M.
LOCATION: Dip. Sci. Farm., Univ. Ferrara, Italy
JOURNAL: Farmaco, Ed. Prat. DATE: 1988 VOLUME: 43 NUMBER: 2 PAGES: 47-55 CODEN: FRPPAO ISSN: 0430-0912 LANGUAGE: Italian

? ss s1/pat

    S6   278   S1/PAT

? t 6/3/1-3

6/3/1

109061458 CA: 109(8)61458w PATENT
A parenterally administrable composition containing coacervate system
INVENTOR(AUTHOR): Ecanow, Bernard
LOCATION: USA
ASSIGNEE: NeoMed Corp.
PATENT: European Pat. Appl. ; EP 256856 A2 DATE: 880224
APPLICATION: EP 87307152 (870813) *US 896844 (860814)
PAGES: 35 pp. CODEN: EPXXDW LANGUAGE: English
CLASS: A61K-009/10A; A61K-009/50B DESIGNATED COUNTRIES: AT; BE; CH; DE; ES; FR; GB; GR; IT; LI; LU; NL; SE

6/3/2

109055233 CA: 109(7)55233c PATENT
Preparation of proline esters and pharmaceutical formulations containing them as drug absorption promoters
   INVENTOR(AUTHOR): Tsuda, Yoko; Sato, Susumu; Komata, Tetsuo
   LOCATION: Japan,
   ASSIGNEE: Nitto Electric Industrial Co., Ltd.
   PATENT: Japan Kokai Tokkyo Koho ; JP 87226930 A2 ; JP 62226930 DATE: 871005
   APPLICATION: JP 8669468 (860327)
   PAGES: 10 pp. CODEN: JKXXAF LANGUAGE: Japanese CLASS: A61K-047/00A

6/3/3

109043454 CA: 109(6)43454n PATENT
Benzodiazepine sedative aerosol preparation and its manufacture
   INVENTOR(AUTHOR): Burghart, Kurt; Burghart, Walter
   LOCATION: Fed. Rep. Ger.
   PATENT: PCT International ; WO 8705210 A1 DATE: 870911
   APPLICATION: WO 87AT15 (870310) *AT 86621 (860310)
   PAGES: 18 pp. CODEN: PIXXD2 LANGUAGE: German CLASS: A61K-009/12A; A61K-031/55B DESIGNATED COUNTRIES: AU; DK; JP; US DESIGNATED REGIONAL: A; BE; CH; DE; FR; GB; IT; LU; NL; SE

? ss s1/npt

    S7   6112   S1/NPT

? t 1/3/1-3

1/3/1

   109061458   CA: 109(8)61458w PATENT
   A parenterally administrable composition containing coacervate system
      INVENTOR(AUTHOR): Ecanow, Bernard
      LOCATION: USA

ASSIGNEE: NeoMed Corp.
PATENT: European Pat. Appl. ; EP 256856 A2 DATE: 880224
APPLICATION: EP 87307152 (870813) *US 896844 (860814)
PAGES: 35 pp. CODEN: EPXXDW LANGUAGE: English CLASS: A61K-009/10A; A61K-009/50B DESIGNATED COUNTRIES: AT; BE; CH; DE; ES; FR; GB; GR; IT; LI; LU; NL; SE

1/3/2

109055233 CA: 109(7)55233c PATENT
Preparation of proline esters and pharmaceutical formulations containing them as drug absorption promoters
INVENTOR (AUTHOR): Tsuda, Yoko; Sato, Susumu; Komata, Tetsuo
LOCATION: Japan
ASSIGNEE: Nitto Electric Industrial Co., Ltd.
PATENT: Japan Kokai Tokkyo Koho ; JP 87226930 A2 ; JP 62226930 DATE: 871005
APPLICATION: JP 8669468 (860327)
PAGES: 10 pp. CODEN: JKXXAF LANGUAGE: Japanese CLASS: A61K-047/00A

1/3/3

109049976 CA: 109(7)49976f JOURNAL
Effect of Lathyrus sativus toxin on cognitive functions and urinary catecholamines in experimental animals
AUTHOR(S): Karanth, K. S.; Madhyastha, M. S.; Aroor, A. R.
LOCATION: Dep. Pharmacol., Kasturba Med. Coll., Manipal, 576119, India
JOURNAL: Indian J. Med. Res. DATE: 1988 VOLUME: 87 NUMBER: May
PAGES: 459-62   CODEN: IJMRAQ ISSN: 0019-5340 LANGUAGE: English

? e pa=pfizer

Ref	Items	Index-term
E1	1	PA=PFISTERER, KARL, ELEKTROTECHNISCHE SPEZIALARTI
E2	1	PA=PFISTERER, KARL, FABRIK ELEKTROTECHNISCHER SPE
E3	1771	*PA=PFIZER
E4	1	PA=PFIZER AB
E5	1	PA=PFIZER CHEMICAL CORP.
E6	206	PA=PFIZER CORP.
E7	3	PA=PFIZER G.M.B.H.
E8	10	PA=PFIZER HOSPITAL PRODUCTS GROUP, INC.
E9	1	PA=PFIZER IN.
E10	1115	PA=PFIZER INC.
E11	156	PA=PFIZER LTD.
E12	3	PA=PFIZER QUIGLEY K. K.

Enter P or E for more

? p

Ref	Items	Index-term
E13	10	PA=PFIZER TAITO CO., LTD.
E14	1	PA=PFIZER, CHAS. + CO., INC.
E15	1	PA=PFIZER, CHAS. AND CO.
E16	1	PA=PFIZER, CHAS. AND CO., INC.
E17	1	PA=PFIZER, CHAS. CO., INC.
E18	2	PA=PFIZER, CHAS., + CO., INC.
E19	2	PA=PFIZER, CHAS., AND CO.
E20	3	PA=PFIZER, CHAS., AND CO. INC.
E21	289	PA=PFIZER, CHAS., AND CO., INC.
E22	3	PA=PFIZER, CHAS, AND CO., INC.
E23	1	PA=PFIZER, CHASI, AND CO , INC.
E24	37	PA=PFIZER, INC.

Enter P or E for more

? e cs=pfizer

Ref	Items	Index-term
E1	2	CS = PFISTERER
E2	1	CS = PFITZER
E3	3365	*CS = PFIZER
E4	3	CS = PFKU
E5	1	CS = PFLANEENSCHUTZ
E6	1	CS = PFLANGENOEKOL
E7	1	CS = PFLANSEN
E8	1	CS = PFLANSENSCHUTZ
E9	399	CS = PFLANZ
E10	3	CS = PFLANZANBAU
E11	1	CS = PFLANZBAU
E12	47	CS = PFLANZE

Enter P or E for more

GENERAL EXERCISES

Not all of these require the use of *Chemical Abstracts*. Some of these questions actually came from patrons of the New York Public Library.

1. Find review articles on supercooled liquids or supercooling of liquid metals.
2. Find a reference after 1981 to the chemical synthesis (preparation) of anthraquinone.
3. Determine the boiling point of benzene.
4. Find a reference to the stability of cocaine.
5. Find references to essential oils obtained from coriander seeds.
6. Find a paper published in early 1988 by Nick Turro of the Columbia University Department of Chemistry.
7. Find references to the toxicity of Agent Orange. Use *CA* and one other source.
8. Find references in STC to the marketing of plastics.
9. Determine which companies currently sell phenol.

10. Use a source other than *Chemical Abstracts* to determine when Valium or Diazepam was first synthesized in the laboratory.

READING LIST

Antony, Arthur. *Guide to basic information sources in chemistry*. New York: J. Norton Publishers: distributed by Halsted Press; 1979. 219p.

Awareness of information sources. Edited by Theodore B. Selover, Jr., and Max Klein. New York: American Institute of Chemical Engineers; 1986. 132p.

Chemical engineering datasources. Edited by Dorothy A. Jankowski and T. B. Selover. New York: American Institute of Chemical Engineers; 1986; 72p.

Maizell, Robert E. *How to find chemical information: a guide for practicing chemists, educators, and students*. New York: J. Wiley; 1987. 402p.

Schulz, Hedda. *From CA to CAS Online*. New York: VCH; 1988. 227p.

Skolnik, Herman. *The literature matrix of chemistry*. New York: Wiley; 1982. 297p.

The use of chemical literature. Edited by R. T. Bottle. [2nd ed., rev.] Hamden, Conn.: Archon Books ; 1971. 294p.

Woodburn, Henry Milton. *Using the chemical literature: a practical guide*. New York: M. Dekker; 1974. 302p.

SPECIAL PAPER

Courses for Special Librarianship Offered in ALA-Accredited Programs in 1987 and Implications for the Education of Science/Technology Librarians

Constance M. Mellott

SUMMARY. A survey was made of the 60 library schools with ALA-accredited programs to determine the extent and types of their courses in special librarianship, in specific types of special libraries, and in specific types of literature. From the survey results it was possible to make an analysis of the extent to which these courses would serve the needs of those interested in science/technology libraries. Statistics are presented on the number and types of courses offered for students concerned with science/technology librarianship.

While much of the education received by prospective science/technology librarians takes place outside of the library school, it is important for both library educators and practitioners to see what

---

Constance M. Mellott is Assistant Professor, School of Library Science, Kent State University, Kent, OH 44242. Her PhD is from the University of Pittsburgh, MA (linguistics) from the University of Pittsburgh, MSLS from Western Reserve University, and BS (physics and mathematics) from Mount Union College.

© 1990 by The Haworth Press, Inc. All rights reserved.

courses in library school programs are available for students planning to specialize in science/technology librarianship.

A starting point might be special librarianship courses, so a study of such courses was begun in 1979 through descriptions in the bulletins from library schools with ALA-accredited programs. This study led to further questions that were not answerable from the bulletins and resulted in the design of a questionnaire which was used in 1980 to survey the then 68 ALA-accredited programs.[1]

By 1987, only 60 accredited programs remained and the survey was repeated in order to determine whether the same pattern still existed for courses in special libraries/librarianship, in specific types of special libraries, and in specific types of literature.

METHODOLOGY

The survey instrument used was the same questionnaire used in the earlier study,[2] with the addition of question 2 (see Figure 1). Because the second questionnaire was so similar to the earlier one, no pretest was carried out.

The first round of questionnaires was sent out in January of 1987, with responses returned from 47 schools. The second round of questionnaires was sent out in April and garnered an additional 9 responses. The four remaining schools were contacted by telephone in the fall of 1987 and early winter of 1988 and full information was received from two of them, along with partial information from a third. Thus, 59 out of the 60 programs are included in the present survey for a 98% rate of response.

COURSES IN SPECIAL LIBRARIANSHIP

The survey in 1980 showed that, of the 68 schools with ALA-accredited programs, 58 (85%) had courses in special librarianship. An earlier survey by Ripin and Kasman found that over 80% of the schools with ALA-accredited programs had such courses during the 1974-75 academic year.[3] The 1987 survey showed that 49 (83%) of the 59 schools which responded had such a course and the school from which no response was received had such a course listed in the

SURVEY OF COURSES OFFERED IN SPECIAL LIBRARIANSHIP

1. Do you offer a course in SPECIAL LIBRARIES or SPECIAL LIBRARIANSHIP?
   yes_____   no_____
2. If no, is the material integrated into other courses? How? (Please explain on reverse side of sheet.)
3. If yes, how often is the course offered?
   every term_____   annually_____   biennially_____
   other (please explain)_____
4. Credit hours (please give number)_____ and check whether
   quarter_____   semester_____   trimester_____
5. What is the name of the course?_____
6. Is the emphasis of the course on:
   a. administration of the special library_____
   b. reference materials used in special libraries_____
   c. survey of various kinds of special libraries_____
   d. other (please specify)_____
7. The course is taught by (check those applicable):
   a. regular full-time faculty_____
   b. adjunct faculty_____
   c. outside specialist_____
   d. other (please specify)_____
8. The following courses for SPECIFIC TYPES OF SPECIAL LIBRARIES or SPECIAL LIBRARIANSHIP (e.g., Art Libraries, Law Librarianship, etc.), are offered: (please list courses).

Course Title	Taught by (a,b,c, or d from #7)	How often offered (see #3)

9. The following courses for SPECIFIC TYPES OF LITERATURES (e.g., Legal Bibliography, Medical Literature, Literature of the Social Sciences, etc.) are offered: (please list courses).

Course Title	Taught by (a,b,c, or d from #7)	How often offered (see #3)

10. Comments_____

Figure 1

its catalog. This would make a total of 50 out of the 60 programs including a course in special librarianship.

Of those schools which do not offer courses in special librarianship, four noted that the topic was covered in other courses. One noted that it was included "in bits and pieces" and two noted an emphasis on function across libraries rather than type of library. Both of these schools, however, had courses in particular types of special librarianship, such as art or law. Another stated that "type of library" courses were not offered because they were already part of what was in existing courses, but that students could choose a type of library for field work.

Thirty-seven schools (76% of those with special library/librarianship courses) offered it annually, four (8%) offered it every term, three (6%) every other term, one every spring and sometimes in the summer, and one once or twice a year depending on the demand. Three schools (6%) offer the course biennially.

In the 1980 survey, 71% of the schools with the course offered it annually; 12% every term; 3% every other term; 5% twice a year; 5% biennially; one offered the course every third semester; one "when feasible"; and one, while the course was planned as an annual offering, had not reached that frequency (see Table 1).

Table 1: Credit Given for Special Libraries/Librarianship Courses

Credit	No. Schools 1980	No. Schools 1987
3 quarter hours	6	2
4 quarter hours	4	2
5 quarter hours	1	1
2 trimester hours	2	--
3 trimester hours	3	2
2 semester hours	2	2
3 semester hours	36	37
4 semester hours	2	1
Other or not stated	2	2

Faculty

Of the 49 schools with special libraries/librarianship courses, 39 (80%) reported use of regular full-time faculty to teach the courses; one additional school reported use of both regular full-time faculty and outside specialists. Five schools (10%) reported use of adjunct faculty; two (4%) use of outside specialists; and one, "regular part-time faculty."

In the 1980 survey, 66% reported use of regular full-time faculty and 12% of regular full-time faculty and outside specialists. One school also used regular part-time faculty. Four (7%) used regular full-time faculty and adjunct faculty. Four (7%) used only adjunct faculty. Three schools using regular full-time faculty also noted the use of guest speakers from the field.

The largest percentage increase to the 1987 survey is the 14% increase in the number of courses taught by full-time faculty (see Table 2).

Table 2: Faculty Teaching Special Libraries/Librarianship Courses

	No. Schools 1980	No. Schools 1987
Regular full-time faculty	38	39
Regular full-time faculty and adjunct faculty	4	--
Regular full-time faculty and outside specialist	7	1
Adjunct faculty	4	5
Outside specialist	1	3
Regular part-time faculty	1	1
Visiting lecturer	1	--
Adjunct faculty and outside specialist	1	--
Regular full-time faculty, adjunct faculty and outside specialist	1	--
Total number of schools	58	49

Content of Special Libraries Courses

Question 6 dealt with the emphasis of the course on special libraries/librarianship. Courses vary from school to school even when the course title is the same, and course descriptions are not always a dependable guide to course emphases and contents. Of the responses from schools with special libraries/librarianship courses, 20 (41%) had checked only "administration of the special library," but 18 (37%) more had it checked in addition to other aspects for a total of 38 (78%). Five others did not check "administration of the special library" but under "other," one noted that "all aspects, but with the most emphasis on management"; another listed "organization and operation of special libraries and information centers"; a third "management, organization, collection, and services. . . . differently in special librarianship"; the fourth, "course integrates management with technical (professional) skills," and the fifth noted that the course included all three listed aspects.

Three schools (6%) had checked only "survey of various kinds of special libraries." Ten others had checked this in combination with other aspects. Only five schools (10%) included "reference materials used in special libraries" with other aspects, but some noted under "other" that all aspects listed in question 6 were included in the course. One school did not respond to this part of the questionnaire (see Table 3).

COURSES FOR SPECIFIC TYPES OF SPECIAL LIBRARIES

Courses listed for specific types of special libraries in Table 4 are those which appeared on more than one questionnaire. Because this section of the questionnaire was open-ended, some respondents omitted course titles that were included in their schools' bulletins. Additionally, many of the courses listed had different courses titles at different schools. Some schools had more than one course for the same specific type of special library. The total number of courses (as opposed to the total number of schools reporting such courses) is

Table 3: Emphases of Special Library/Librarianship Courses

Course Emphases	Number Reporting
A. Administration of the special library	20
C. Survey of various kinds of special libraries	3
A. Administration of the special library, and B. Reference materials used in special libraries	1
A. Administration of the special library, and C. Survey of various kinds of special libraries	6
A. Administration of the special library, B. Reference materials used in special libraries, and C. Survey of various kinds of special libraries	2
A. Administration of the special library, and D. Other	7
A. Administration of the special library, B. Reference materials used in special libraries, C. Survey of various kinds of special libraries, and D. Other	2
D. Other	7
No response	1

shown enclosed in parentheses immediately after the number of schools reporting such courses.

Some of the courses reported by only one school are: Audiovisual Services in Libraries, Libraries Services to Ethnic Communities, Library Services to the Handicapped, Visual Arts Librarianship, and Audiovisual Services in Libraries.

A majority of the courses were listed as being offered annually and were listed as taught by adjunct faculty or outside specialists.

No specific science/technology librarianship courses were included in the responses to this section of the questionnaire.

COURSES FOR SPECIFIC TYPES OF LITERATURE

Question 9 was also open-ended and received a great many different course titles among the responses. Table 5 includes only those types of literature for which at least 15 responses were tabulated. Similar course titles were grouped together for the tabulation.

Table 4: Courses for Specific Types of Special Libraries Reported by More Than One School

Type	Number Reported 1980	1987
Archives	5	10
Art	5	5
Biomedical, Medical, and Health Sciences	42	32 (33)
Law	26	22 (26)
Map	3	2
Music	12	12 (13)
Rare books, Special Collections, and Historical Collections	8	4
Records Management	--	4
Special Groups, Library Services to/for	2	2
Theology	2	1

Note: Numbers in parentheses are the total number of courses. Some schools reported more than one course.

Some of the other course titles appearing in the responses were: Africana Research Resources; Canadian Collections; Ethnic Collections and Publications; Information Sources in Religion; International Information Sources and Services; Latin American Research Resources; Literature of the Fine Arts; Literature of the Performing Arts; Maps as Reference, Research and Information Sources; Materials and Sources for Minority Groups; Slavic Bibliography; and Visual Resources Collections.

A majority of the courses offered in the literatures of the humanities, social sciences, science/technology, and in government documents were reported as being offered at least once a year and taught by regular, full-time faculty.

No responses listed more than one science/technology course, whereas in 1980, three did so. The percentage of schools with science/technology literature courses has increased slightly from 90% in 1980 to 92% in 1987. Ripin and Kasman reported that in 1974-75, 95% of the accredited programs had a science/technology litera-

Table 5: Courses Reported for Specific Types of Literature by Fifteen or More Schools

Type of Percentage Literature	No. Schools Reporting 1980	No. Schools Reporting 1987	Additional Schs. from Bulletins 1980	Additional Schs. from Bulletins 1987	Total No. in 1980	Total No. in 1987
Biomedical, medical and health sciences	32	29 (30)	--	3	32	32
Business	18	25	--	2	18	27
Government Documents/ Publications	27	21 (23)	8	4	35	25
Humanities*	51	45 (47)	7	7	58	52
Legal Bibliography	33	28 (29)	--	6	33	34
Science/ Technology	55	48	6	7	61	55
Social Sciences*	54	44	5	7	59	51

* Includes a combined course for humanities and social sciences reported by four schools (in both the 1980 and 1987 surveys).

NOTE: Numbers in parentheses are for the total number of courses. Some schools reported more than one course.

---

ture course and that 12 schools had more than one such course.[4] Both the 1980 and 1987 figures show decreases from the 1974-75 data.

ONLINE SCIENCE/TECHNOLOGY DATABASE INSTRUCTION

Of the 48 science/technology literature courses reported in the responses, only one was specifically titled as an online course: "On-line Data Banks in Science and Technology." A check of the bulletin from the school which listed that course title did not show any other science/technology literature courses.

No question specifically relating to online courses or online components of courses was included in the questionnaire, but Harter and Fenichel reported finding "consciousness raising" instruction as a component of a variety of library school courses in a 1980 survey including some courses in the literature of science and technology.[5] Accordingly, when the online course appeared in the responses, school bulletins were checked for course descriptions to determine the presence or absence of an online component (at any level) in the science/technology course descriptions. Of those bulletins which were available to be checked, five mentioned such a component while 24 failed to do so. Another survey would be required to determine the actual situation because course descriptions may differ from the actual content of courses being offered.

FIELD WORK

Seven schools noted in the comment section of the questionnaire that field work or internships or practica were available as part of the educational program for special librarianship. In the 1980 survey, seven questionnaires also had similar comments.[6] There was no specific question relating to fieldwork in the questionnaires for either survey.

CONCLUSION

The areas of special library education best developed in ALA-accredited programs still appear to be medical and health sciences librarianship and law librarianship. These areas have type of library courses, type of literature courses, and additional related courses. No separate course for science/technology librarianship was reported.

Students interested in specializing in science/technology librarianship within a library school program may find their specialization limited to special libraries/librarianship (83% of the programs) and/or science/technology literature (93% of the programs and 98% of the programs which included special libraries/librarianship courses). It is also possible in some programs to gain some supervised practical experience through field work or a practicum. There is no major change from the situation reported in the earlier survey for students interested in education for science/technology librarianship.

NOTES

1. Mellott, Constance M. Courses for special librarianship offered in ALA-accredited programs and implications for the education of science/technology librarians. *Science & Technology Libraries*. 1(3): 13-20; 1981 Spring.
2. Mellott, Constance M. *Op. Cit.* p. 14, Figure 1.
3. Ripin, Arley L.; Kasman, Dorothy. Education for special librarianship; a survey of courses offered in accredited programs. *Special Libraries*. 67(11): 504-509; 1976 November.
4. Ripin, Arley L.; Kasman, Dorothy. *Op. Cit.* p. 508, Table 2.
5. Harter, Stephen P.; Fenichel, Carol H. Online searching in library education. *Journal of Education for Librarianship*. 23(1): 3-22; 1982 Summer.
6. Mellott, Constance M. *Op. Cit.* p. 18-19.

SCI-TECH COLLECTIONS

Tony Stankus, Editor

The general public has by now heard much about the technological race the United States is running with the Japanese in the field of superconductivity, the creation of materials whose electrical resistance is so low that many new applications are now possible. Important though this race may be, another contest may be just as vital to this country's position in the field of engineering and science, the field of supercomputers. They are computers whose design allows them to operate at tremendously high speeds. Until recently American computer manufacturers more or less had the field to themselves, but within the past three or four years Japanese firms have begun to enter the market.

This paper by Melvin G. DeSart identifies the important printed and online sources for information on this subject. It is a timely topic.

Information Sources in Supercomputing and Supercomputers

Melvin G. DeSart

SUMMARY. Supercomputing is a relatively new field but its impact is being felt in almost every science and engineering discipline as well as a number of research areas not generally associated with computing. The advent of faster, more powerful computers has made possible arithmetic and design calculations that ten years ago were either impossible, prohibitively expensive, or time consuming. As supercomputers and their applications become more commonplace, demand for information concerning them will increase. This paper presents a brief background on supercomputing and supercomputers followed by a bibliography of references sources in sections covering monographs, monographic series, conference proceedings, journals, indexes and abstracts, online databases, and research centers.

WHAT MAKES THEM "SUPER"

All computers are made up of three basic components: the central processing unit(s) (CPUs), memory and storage, and input/output devices. Two other components must also be considered, however. Without software (the programs that run on the computer) and proper communications equipment to relay information to and from the input/output devices, computers are nothing more than expensive boxes full of electronics. What makes a supercomputer "super" is the optimization of all five of these components.

The CPU (sometimes just called the processor) is the heart of the

---

Melvin G. DeSart is Assistant Engineering Librarian and Assistant Professor of Library Administration at the University of Illinois at Urbana-Champaign, Urbana, IL 61801. He has the BA and MA (Library and Information Science) degrees from the University of Illinois.

© 1990 by The Haworth Press, Inc. All rights reserved.

computer. It is the device that actually *does* the calculations that a program requires. Processors used in supercomputers are the fastest available. They are capable of Millions of (FLoating point) OPerations per Second which is why performance criteria for supercomputer processors are measured in megaflops or MFLOPS. One of the ways these incredible speeds have been reached is by vectorizing the processors. Regular processors use scalar arithmetic. If asked to solve 1000 equations each involving one addition, one subtraction, one multiplication, and one division, a scalar processor will solve each equation one at a time, storing a result as each equation is completed. A vector processor, on the other hand, uses vector arithmetic. A vector processor will take all 1000 equations, solve all of the additions virtually simultaneously, follow by solving all of the subtractions, multiplications, and divisions, then store all 1000 results. Solving equations using vector processing greatly increases the operating speed of supercomputers over that of mainframes that have traditionally used scalar processors.

Another tactic used to increase the speed and power at which supercomputers operate is to increase the number of processors available to do the work. There is a growing trend toward using multiple processors in supercomputers, with each processor able to work on a separate portion of a program. This division of labor among processors is known as parallel processing and offers marked speed increases for those programs that can be structured to take advantage of it. However, many programmers are not accustomed to writing programs for machines that offer parallel processing capabilities. Thus, much of the speed advantage available via parallel processing has not yet been fully utilized.

The processors mentioned above are capable of operating at tremendous speeds, but not without adequate memory from which to draw and store information. Most supercomputers use multiple forms of memory, hierarchically arranged. The most readily accessed storage is the active memory of the supercomputer itself. Other active memory may be added externally in the form of a huge block of memory chips, called a solid-state storage device, or SSD. Active memory is never used for final storage. Its function is to store all intermediate calculations whose results will be needed by the processors at various points in a particular program. The next levels of memory are generally multiple forms of large magnetic disks, some with high-speed transfer to and from the processors, while others, generally with a very high storage capacity, must be accessed at a rate which markedly slows final processing time. The final level of storage is most often magnetic tape, although not generally in the large spool format made popular in films and television.

Having a supercomputer that can calculate at incredibly high speeds is a wonderful thing, but the advantages of the high computing speeds would be quite diluted without a mechanism for getting information into and out of the supercomputer at a proportionally high rate of speed. This is the job of the input/output, or I/O, devices. The I/O device can be thought of as a traffic cop, directing information to and from storage, external input and output, and the processors. The I/O devices are the means by which programs and data enter the supercomputer from the programmer or researcher. With most supercomputers, standard I/O devices are not capable of information transfer rates remotely approaching the available processing rates. Therefore, smaller computers, called minicomputers or superminicomputers, are used as I/O devices to control the flow of information in and out of the larger machines.

Connecting all of the pieces together is the job of the communications equipment. If the I/O devices are the traffic cops of a supercomputer, the communications equipment is the maze of streets along which the traffic flows. Inadequate communications equipment causes delays in transmission of data from one element of the supercomputer to another element or to an outside source. This delay or lack of quality in transmission degrades the total performance of the system as easily as inferior memory or an inferior processor. Clean, high speed data channels connecting the processors, memory, and I/O devices routinely transmit data at 50 to 100 million bits per second. Smaller, lower capacity lines link the supercomputer to minicomputers that control printers, other output devices, and transmission of data to off-site locations. Finally, communications lines that transmit from 56 kilobits per second to approximately 1 megabit per second handle communications between the supercomputer center and off-site researchers.

The final component that determines whether a computer is "super" or not is the programming. Optimizing performance of a supercomputer requires optimization of the software that determines the order in which operations are performed by the hardware. Increases in system speed may be gained by tailoring the software to match the strengths of the hardware. In other words, supercomputer software is made "super" by taking the greatest advantage of the "super" properties of the hardware. Vectorizing a program means writing the code so as to take the greatest advantage of the vector processors available in the supercomputer. If a machine has multiple processors, a programmer can increase the performance of the machine by structuring his code to allow different processors to work on different portions of the program at the same time. Multiple processors used in this manner are known as parallel processors and code written to take advantage of this hardware structure is known as parallel programming.

Past

In the fifties and early sixties, the largest most powerful computers available were those now labelled mainframes. These computers were large, expensive, general purpose machines with the most powerful processors and greatest memories available and were manufactured by companies such as Control Data Corporation (CDC), Digital Equipment Corporation (DEC), and International Business Machines (IBM). IBM made two attempts to develop a supercomputer in the late fifties and sixties, but both met with failure. Finally, in the mid-sixties, supercomputers achieved their own identity when the Control Data Corporation released its CDC 6600. This machine was more powerful and faster than any machine previously sold commercially, but it was also much more expensive; so expensive, in fact, that only specialized government agencies, a few aerospace and petroleum companies, and a small number of universities could justify the expense of purchasing one. In 1972, Seymour Cray, principle designer of CDC's 6600 and 7600 supercomputer, left Control Data to form Cray Research Inc. in Chippewa Falls, Wisconsin. Results came four years later when Cray's first product, the Cray-1, entered the supercomputing market. Cray's machine outperformed any CDC product available at the time, but was even more expensive than any of CDC's machines. The U.S. government was willing to take a chance on the new product, however, and purchased the $13 million machine for the Los Alamos National Laboratory in Santa Fe, New Mexico. A superior product and a buyer were all that Cray needed to enter the market against CDC, and now he had both. Control Data, now realizing that they had a legitimate challenge to their hold on the supercomputing market, began intensive research to develop a machine that could outperform the Cray-1. The battle was joined. The period from 1976 to about 1984 was filled with constant one-upsmanship as first Cray, then CDC, released increasingly faster and more powerful machines. As the supercomputing market increased, so did the number of companies producing machines. In 1985, three Japanese firms, Fujitsu, NEC, and Hitachi, all began delivering supercomputers in Japan. All three companies also began attempting to dent the U.S. market, but to date have met with only modest success. At this same time, IBM also reentered the market, offering their top of the line mainframes with attached vector processors.

Present

Current demand for supercomputer access is at an all-time high. As each new supercomputer comes on line, requests for computing time quickly fill most machines to near capacity. Supercomputer access is available at most large universities and in a growing number of companies in the U.S. and Japan, but many of these facilities are struggling to meet the time demands on their machines. In the marketplace, Cray is still the sales leader in the U.S., followed by Control Data, with IBM a distant third. Fujitsu, NEC, and Hitachi still sell most of their machines in Japan. Worldwide, supercomputer demand is growing, with all six companies mentioned above fighting for a share of the market.

Future

What's ahead? Use of parallel programming and parallel processing will most likely increase dramatically. Applications that call specifically for graphics or near-supercomputer power and speed without a supercomputer's price tag will increase substantially the graphics supercomputer and minisupercomputer markets. As the limits of current technology are reached, new technologies will surface to expand the limits of supercomputing even further. For example, current circuit chips are made with a base structure of silicon. Silicon chips produce heat as electrical currents run through the circuits built onto the chips. This production of heat is a great concern to supercomputer manufacturers, necessitating complex cooling mechanisms to prevent the machines from overheating, and limiting the density at which chips may be concentrated inside the machines. New chip technologies, using the compound gallium arsenide as a base material, greatly reduce the production of heat in the machines, thus improving their efficiency. The Cray-3, to be released sometime during 1989, will be the first supercomputer to employ gallium arsenide technology. The number of applications for which supercomputers can be used is large now and increasing rapidly. One can only assume that a corresponding increase in resource materials will follow closely behind, welcoming a new and larger audience into the world of the supercomputer.

RESOURCE TOOLS

Library of Congress Subject Headings

Cataloged materials concerning supercomputers and supercomputing may be found under the term "Supercomputers" while the oldest material may be found under "Electronic Digital Computers." Related terms of interest are "Parallel Processing (Electronic Computers)," "Parallel Programming (Computer Science)," and "Multiprocessors," while the only narrower term available at the present is "CYBER 205 (Computer)."

Call Number Classifications

Dewey: Current material on supercomputers is classed at 004.11 if the emphasis is on data processing or computer science and at 621.3911 if the emphasis is on computer engineering. Materials on programming supercomputers are classed at 005.21 while materials dealing with programs for supercomputers are classed at 005.31.

Library of Congress: All materials should be classed at QA76.5.

Serial and Monographic Tools

Books in Print lists currently available materials under the heading: "Supercomputers." *Ulrich's International Periodicals Directory* lists journals dealing with supercomputing under: "Computers" and "Computers—Software."

MONOGRAPHS

The works in this section will be broken down into three categories: popularizations, general, and research. Included in this section will be monographs and works that are compilations of *selected* papers from conferences or other sources. The field of supercomputing is so new (approximately 1975 to date) that only in the last 4 to 5 years has the monographic material available in this area appeared in quantity. A fortunate byproduct of the currency of the material is that most of it is still in print and thus still accessible for most libraries and information centers.

Popularizations

Three works have appeared to date:

Carter, Alden R.; LeBlanc, Wayne J. *Supercomputers*. New York: F. Watts; 1985.
Darling, David J. *Fast, faster, fastest: the story of supercomputers*. Minneapolis, MN: Dillon Press; 1986.
Packard, Edward *Supercomputer*. New York: Bantam; 1984.

General

Some of the works listed here will deal with supercomputing in layman's terms, including government reports and hearings, while others will be more readily understood by an audience with at least some knowledge of computer science.

Hwang, Kai, ed. *Supercomputers: design and applications*. Silver Spring, MD: IEEE Computer Society; 1984.
Infotech. *Super-computers*. (Infotech State of the Art Report). Maidenhead, England: Infotech; 1979. 2 vols.

Jenkins, Richard A. *Supercomputers of today and tomorrow: the parallel processing revolution*. Blue Ridge Summit, PA: Tab Books; 1986.

Karin, Sidney; Smith, Norris Parker. *The supercomputer era*. Boston: Harcourt Brace Jovanovich; 1987.

Kirkland, J.R.; Poore, J.H., eds. *Supercomputers: a key to U.S. scientific, technological, and industrial preeminence*. New York: Praeger; 1987.

Lazou, Christopher. *Supercomputers and their use*. Rev. ed. New York: Oxford University Press; 1988.

Simons, G. L. *Towards fifth-generation computers*. Manchester, England: NCC Publications; 1983.

United States. Congress. House. Committee on Science and Technology. *Supercomputers*. Washington: U.S. Government Printing Office; 1984.

United States. Congress. House. Committee on Science and Technology. Subcommittee on Energy Development and Applications. *Federal supercomputer programs and policies*. Washington: U.S. Government Printing Office; 1986.

United States. Congress. Office of Technology Assessment. *Supercomputers: government plans and policies: background paper*. Washington: U.S. Government Printing Office; 1986.

Research

Banerjee, Uptal. *Dependence analysis for supercomputing*. (Kluwer International Series in Engineering and Computer Science. Parallel Processing and Fifth Generation Computing). Boston, MA: Kluwer Academic; 1988.

Business Communications Staff. *Supercomputers: materials, components, software*. Norwalk, CT: Business Communications Co.; 1986.

Fernbach, Sidney, ed. *Supercomputers: class VI systems, hardware, and software*. New York: Elsevier Science Pub. Co.; 1986.

Hord, R. Michael. *The Illiac IV, the first supercomputer*. Rockville, MD: Computer Science Press; 1982.

Hwang, Kai; DeGroot, Douglas, eds. *Parallel processing for su-

percomputers and artificial intelligence. New York: McGraw-Hill; 1989.

Jensen, Klavs F.; Truhlar, eds. *Supercomputer research in chemistry and chemical engineering*. (ACS Symposium Series; 353). Washington, DC: American Chemical Society; 1987.

Kowalik, J.S., ed. *Parallel MIMD computation: the HEP supercomputer and its applications*. (MIT Press Series in Scientific Computation). Cambridge, MA: MIT Press; 1985.

Kuwahara, K., et al., eds. *Supercomputers and fluid dynamics*. (Lecture Notes in Engineering; 24). New York: Springer-Verlag; 1986.

Levesque, John M.; Williamson, Joel W. *A guidebook to Fortran on supercomputers*. San Diego, CA: Academic Press; 1988.

Lykos, Peter; Shavitt, Isiah, eds. *Supercomputers in chemistry*. (ACS Symposium Series; 173). Washington, DC: American Chemical Society; 1981.

McCormick, S.F., ed. *Multigrid methods: theory, applications, and supercomputing*. (Lecture Notes in Pure and Applied Mathematics; 110). New York: M. Dekker; 1988.

Mendez, R.H. *Japanese supercomputing: architecture, algorithms, and applications*. (Lecture Notes in Engineering; 36) New York: Springer-Verlag; 1988.

Ortega, James M. *Introduction to parallel and vector solution of linear systems*. (Frontiers of Computer Science). New York: Plenum Press; 1988.

Paddon, D.J., ed. *Supercomputers and parallel computation*. (The Institute of Mathematics and its Applications Conference Series; new ser., 1) (Oxford Science Series). New York: Oxford University Press; 1984.

Schneck, Paul B. *Supercomputer architecture*. (Kluwer International Series in Engineering and Computer Science. Parallel Processing and Fifth Generation Computing). Boston: Kluwer Academic; 1987.

Society of Automotive Engineers. *Automotive applications of supercomputers*. (SAE Special Publication; 708). Warrendale, PA: Society of Automotive Engineers; 1988.

Society of Automotive Engineers. *Supercomputers in the automo-

tive industry. (SAE Special Publication; 624). Warrendale, PA: Society of Automotive engineers; 1985.

Wilhelmson, Robert B., ed. *High speed computing: scientific applications and algorithm design.* Urbana, IL: University of Illinois Press; 1988.

MONOGRAPHIC SERIES

Two monographic series are currently being produced that deal specifically with supercomputing and supercomputers.

McGraw-Hill Series in Supercomputing and Artificial Intelligence. New York: McGraw-Hill.
   To date, two titles have appeared in this series.

Quinn, Michael J. *Designing efficient algorithms for parallel computers.* 1987.

Wiederhold, Gio. *File organization for database design.* 1987.

Special topics in computing. New York: Elsevier Science Pub. Co.
   Four volumes are currently available in this series.

Dongarra, J.J., ed. *Experimental parallel computing architectures.* v.1, 1987.

Martin, Joanne L., ed. *Performance evaluation of supercomputers.* v.4. 1988.

Schonauer, Willi. *Scientific computing on vector computers.* v.2, 1987.

te Riele, H.J.J.; Dekker, Th. J.; van der Horst, H.A., eds. *Algorithms and applications on vector and parallel computers.* v.3, 1987.

A number of other series produce occasional volumes dealing with supercomputing, generally with a thrust toward a particular application.

ACS Symposium Series. Washington, DC: American Chemical Society.

Bochumer Schriften zur Paralleten Datenverarbeitung. Bochum, Germany: Rechenzentrum der Rhur-Universitat Bochum; 12 n1, 1987.

Lecture Notes in Computer Science. New York: Springer-Verlag; v.297, 1988.

Lecture Notes in Engineering. New York: Springer-Verlag; v.36, 1988.

Society of Automotive Engineers, Special Publications. Warrendale, PA: Society of Automotive Engineers; v.708, 1988.

CONFERENCE PROCEEDINGS

The byword when considering conferences dealing with supercomputing is diversity. As more and more scientific and engineering research areas and organizations become aware of the potential that supercomputing holds, the more conferences that are held considering supercomputing and its applications within a specific discipline. The proceedings listed below will be broken into two groups; those that are held on a recurring basis, for which a generic entry will be listed under the name of the conference, and unique symposia, for which full information concerning a particular conference will be listed.

Recurring

Conference on Supercomputers and Applications. Bochum, Germany: Rechenzentrum der rhur-Universitat Bochum; 10th-, 1986-.

International Conference on Supercomputing Systems. Washington, DC: IEEE Computer Society Press; 1st-, 1985-.

Supercomputer Applications Symposium. New York: Plenum Press; 4th-, 1985-.

Supercomputers and Fluid Dynamics: Proceedings of the Nobeyama Workshop. New York: Springer-Verlag; 1st-, 1985-.
Supercomputing. New York: Springer-Verlag; 1st-, 1987-.
Supercomputing. Washington, DC: IEEE Computer Society Press; 1st-, 1988-.

Unique

Cornwell, T.J., ed. *The Use of Supercomputers in Observational Astronomy: Proceedings of a Workshop*; 1985; Minneapolis, MN. Green Bank, WV: National Radio Astronomy Observatory; 1988. (NRAO Workshop Proceedings; 15).
Devreese, Jozef T.; Van Camp, Piet, eds. *International Workshop on the Use of Supercomputers on Theoretical Science. Supercomputers in Theoretical and Experimental Science*; 1984; Priorij Corsendonk, Belgium. New York: Plenum Press; 1985.
Dupuis, Michel, ed. *Symposium on Supercomputer Chemistry;* 1985; Montreal, Quebec. New York: Springer-Verlag; 1987. (Lecture Notes in Chemistry; 44).
Emmen, A.H.L., ed. *International Supercomputer Applications Symposium*; 1984; Amsterdam, Netherlands. New York: Elsevier Science Pub. Co.; 1985.
Hut, P.; McMillan, S., eds. *The Use of Supercomputers in Stellar Dynamics: Proceedings of a Workshop*; 1986; Princeton, NJ. New York: Springer-Verlag; 1986. (Lecture Notes in Physics; 267).
Kamat, Manohar P., ed. *Super and Parallel Computers and their Impact on Civil Engineering: Proceedings of a Session at Structures '86*; 1986; New Orleans, LA. New York: American Society of Civil Engineers; 1986.
Lichnewsky, A.; Saquez, C., eds. *Supercomputers: State-of-the-art.* New York. Elsevier Science Pub. Co.; 1987.
Marino, C., ed. *International Conference on Supercomputer Applications in the Automotive Industry*; 1986; Zurich, Switzerland. Southampton, England: Computational Mechanics; 1986.
Matsen, F.A.; Tajima, T., eds. *Supercomputers: Algorithms, Architectures, and Scientific Computation*; 1985; Austin, TX; Uni-

versity of Texas at Austin. Austin: University of Texas Press; 1986.

Metropolis, N.; et al., eds. *Frontiers of Supercomputing*; 1983; Berkeley, CA. Berkeley, CA: University of California Press; 1986.

Murman, Earll M.; Abarbanel, Saul S., eds. *Progress and Supercomputing in Computational Fluid Dynamics: Proceedings of a U.S.-Israel Workshop*: 1984. Boston: Birkhauser; 1985. (Progress in Scientific Computing; 6).

Winters, Stephen; Schumny, Harald, eds. *Supercomputers: Technology and Applications: 14th EUROMICRO Symposium on Microprocessing and Microprogramming (EUROMICRO '88)*; 1988; Zurich, Switzerland. New York: Elsevier Science Pub. Co.; 1988.

JOURNALS

One look at the publication history of journals dealing specifically with supercomputing and supercomputers illustrates both the currency of the topic and the sudden, large increase in interest in the area. Until 1984, the only journals covering supercomputing were house organs of supercomputer manufacturers and had controlled circulation, such as *Cray Channels* from Cray Research, Inc. Articles dealing with supercomputer hardware, and to a lesser extent software, appeared in existing computer journals. Articles dealing with supercomputer applications and their associated software tended to be published in journals whose focus was the area to which the supercomputer was being applied, e.g. engineering, physics, astronomy, chemistry, etc. In 1984, supercomputing began to carve out a niche in the journal literature with the publication of the first issue of *Supercomputer*, a European journal from a supercomputing center in Amsterdam. Finally, in 1987, not one, but three new supercomputing journals began publication. The journals listed below are those dealing specifically with supercomputers and their applications. Literally hundreds of other scientific and technical journals, far too many to list here, occasionally publish articles on new supercomputer hardware, software, or applications. These may best be found by searching appropriate indexes, abstracts, and online databases.

Cray Channels. Minneapolis, MN: Cray Research; v.1-; 1979?-.

International Journal of Supercomputer Applications. Cambridge, MA: MIT Press; v.1-; 1987-.

Journal of Supercomputing. Boston: Kluwer Academic Publishers; v.1-; 1987-.

Supercomputer. Amsterdam, Netherlands: Amsterdam Universities Computing Centre; v.1-; 1984-.

SuperComputing. Sunnyvale, CA: Supercomputing Magazine; 1987-.

INDEXES AND ABSTRACTS

A number of indexing and abstracting tools yield successful results when searching for information on supercomputing. However, because of the current nature of the topic, not all indexes and abstracts that reference supercomputing literature have appropriate subject headings to make searching easier, more comprehensive, or more efficient. In many cases, searches of the online equivalents of these print sources, where available, will prove more successful. Many other indexes and abstracts, especially those in the physical sciences and engineering, will reference materials dealing with applications of supercomputing in the subject areas covered by those tools. Those indexes and abstracts will not be included here. Anyone interested in locating material on supercomputing applications in a particular subject area is advised to investigate indexing and abstracting tools in that subject area as well as those listed below.

Applied Science and Technology Index. New York: H.W. Wilson Co., V.1-; 1958-.

> A surprisingly good index for popular literature on supercomputing. *ASTI*'s coverage of many popular business periodicals makes it a very good source for information on the business end of the supercomputing industry rather than on the theoretical or technical aspects of the industry. Headings include "Su-

percomputers" as well as a number of headings dealing with specific machines, such as Crays or Cybers.

CMCI: CompuMath Citation Index. Philadelphia, PA: Institute for Scientific Information, 1976-.
ISI's index of computer science and mathematics offers a Citation Index for following the impact of particular authors or research areas in the industry via bibliographies. The Permuterm Subject Index offers keyword access for article titles. Also available as an online file. (See listing under "Online Databases").

Computer Abstracts. St. Helier, Jersey, British Channel Islands: Technical Information Company Ltd., v.1-; 1957-.
Published monthly. Covers articles and papers from journals, conference proceedings, etc., U.S. government reports, and books. *Computer Abstracts* does not have a heading that specifically addresses supercomputing.

Computer and Control Abstracts. Piscataway, NJ: INSPEC/IEEE, v.1-; 1966-.
Published monthly with semi-annual indexes plus 4 year index cumulations. An excellent source for information in computer science. However, *Computer and Control Abstracts* does not have a specific heading which addresses supercomputing literature. An investigation of a series of current monthly issues located supercomputing articles under at least a dozen different subject headings. More complete (and less frustrating) search results may be obtained by searching the INSPEC database of which *Computer and Control Abstracts* is a part. (See listing under "Online Databases").

Computing Reviews. New York: Association for Computing Machinery, v.1-; 1960-.
Published monthly. *Computing Reviews* is neither an abstract nor an index, but rather a review journal. It covers all areas of computer science and computer engineering as they apply to disciplines in both the arts and sciences. *Computing Reviews* does not have a specific heading for supercomputing, but ma-

terials may be found under the classification C.5.1, Large and Medium ("Mainframe") Computers.

Engineering Index. New York: Engineering Information Inc., v.1-; 1884-.
Published monthly, with annual indexes and 3-year index cumulations, *Engineering Index* offers coverage of a broad range of engineering disciplines. Supercomputing literature covered deals mainly with engineering applications with some coverage of hardware and software. The abstracts do not offer a heading for supercomputers, but the subject index, introduced in 1987, does, making materials from 1987 forward much more accessible than materials abstracted prior to 1987. Materials abstracted prior to 1987 are more readily obtained through *EI*'s online counterparts, "Compendex" and "Compendex Plus." (See listing under "Online Databases").

Government Reports Announcements and Index. Springfield, VA: National Technical Information Service, v.1-; 1946-.
Published bi-weekly with monthly and annual keyword, author, corporate author, contract and grant number, and report number indexes. Many of the scientific and engineering applications of supercomputers are subsidized through government contracts. This makes *GRAI* a index worthy of scrutiny for literature on supercomputing. *GRAI*'s broad subject classification does not offer a heading for supercomputers, but with the availability of a keyword index, access to the appropriate literature is not a problem. Available online as "NTIS." (See listing under "Online Databases").

ONLINE DATABASES

With the vast amount of information being produced today and the time constraints on those who need access to that information, the availability of online databases is, in many cases, the only viable information access option open to some researchers. Online databases offer fast, comprehensive coverage of information that may have been scattered throughout various areas of a printed index. Access to these online databases is not free, but, in many cases, the cost of an online search is worth the time saved in searching printed indexes and abstracts. Online databases also offer the advantage of more timely access to material than can printed indexes and abstracts. This is especially important in "hot" areas such as supercomputing, where material is being produced at such a prolific rate. Just as in the case of the printed indexes and abstracts, the databases listed are those that directly cover materials on supercomputing and supercomputers. Appropriate databases should be consulted when dealing with supercomputing applications in a particular subject area.

Computer and Mathematics Search (CMCI). Philadelphia, PA: Institute for Scientific Information, 1980-.
  CMCI is the electronic equivalent of *CMCI: CompuMath Citation Index* and is available only on BRS.

Compendex and *Compendex Plus*. New York: Engineering Information Inc., 1970-.
  Compendex is an electronic equivalent of *Engineering Index*, while *Compendex Plus* is *Compendex* plus an online version of the index *Engineering Meetings*. *Compendex* is available on BRS and STN, while *Compendex Plus* is available on Dialog. *MEET*, the equivalent of *Engineering Meetings*, is available separately on STN.

Computer Database. Belmont, CA: Information Access Co., 1983-.
  This database has no print equivalent. This database concentrates on coverage of hardware and software, as well as some coverage of the business aspects of computers, software, and their applications. The *Computer Database* also contains product evaluations plus profiles and financial information for companies in the computer industry. This database is available through BRS and Dialog.

INSPEC. London: Institution of Electrical Engineers, 1969-.
  INSPEC is an online equivalent of *Computer and Control Abstracts*, referenced previously, plus *Electrical and Electronic Abstracts* and *Physics Abstracts*. A marked advantage over

searching the printed versions because of their lack of pertinent subject headings in the paper copies. Available in BRS, Dialog (split into two files), and STN.

NTIS. Springfield, VA: National Technical Information Service, 1964-.
This equivalent to *Government Reports Announcements and Index* is available through BRS, Dialog, and STN.

Table 1 illustrates graphically a number of points mentioned previously in connection with the literature of supercomputing and supercomputers. A comparison of sets A and C show the obvious lack of appropriate subject headings in both Compendex Plus and IN-

TABLE 1

Feb. 15, 1989 Search Postings

for "Supercomput" in Selected Databases

A = Set A, "Supercomput" truncated, over entire database.

B = Set A limited to title, descriptor, and identifier fields.

C = Set A limited to descriptor field only.

D = Set A limited to 1980 to date.

E = Set A limited to 1988 to date.

	A	B	C	D	E
CMCI	598	NA	NA	598	206
Compendex +	797	581	0	783	67
Computer Db	1651	1158	1070	1651	510
INSPEC (77-)	1420	1190	0	1391	315
NTIS	525	387	281	511	52

SPEC. Comparison of sets A vs. D and of the results from the INSPEC backfile vs. the current INSPEC file shows the currentness of supercomputing literature. The materials on supercomputing tend to be clustered in the period from 1980 to date. Set E shows that the amount of supercomputing literature shows every sign of increasing, rather than levelling off or decreasing.

RESEARCH CENTERS

Given the recent surge in interest in supercomputing, it should not be surprising that supercomputing centers are being established all over the U.S. and Japan, as well as in Canada and western Europe. Most of the centers that offer access to outside users are affiliated with universities, university consortiums, or government organizations. Many large corporations and companies also own supercomputers or minisupercomputers, but access to many of these is limited to researchers within the companies themselves or to selected affiliates. The number of centers just in the U.S. alone has become prohibitively large to list here. What follows is a list of the five supercomputer centers in the U.S. that were established with the assistance of large grants from the National Science Foundation. The NSF offers a large percentage of the available computer time at these centers to projects that are submitted as grant requests. The remaining time is allocated by the centers, a portion to university affiliated requests, and a portion to private firms.

Center for Theory and Simulation in Science and Engineering/Cornell National Supercomputer Facility (CNSF)
Theory Center
265 Olin Hall
Cornell University
Ithaca, NY 14853

John von Neumann Center for Scientific Computing (JVNC)
Consortium for Scientific Computing
P.O. Box 3717
665 College Road East
Princeton, NJ 08543

National Center for Supercomputing Applications (NCSA)
University of Illinois at Urbana-Champaign
152 Computing Applications Bldg.
605 E. Springfield Ave.
Champaign, IL 61820

Pittsburgh Supercomputing Center (PSC)
4400 Fifth Ave.
409C Mellon Institute
Pittsburgh, PA 15213

San Diego Supercomputer Center (SDSC)
GA Technologies, Inc.
P.O. Box 85608
San Diego, CA 92138

Anyone wishing to sample the literature on supercomputing or supercomputers is encouraged to examine Karin and Smith's *The Supercomputer Era*, referenced as a general work in the *books* section above. The book is light, witty, and entertaining while also being quite informative.

REFERENCES

Karin, Sidney; Smith, Norris Parker. *The supercomputer era*. New York: Harcourt Brace Jovanovich; 1987.

Lazou, Christopher. *Supercomputers and their uses*. New York: Oxford University Press; 1986.

Perry, Tekla S.; Zorpette, Glenn. Supercomputer experts predict expansive growth, *IEEE Spectrum*. 26-33; 1989 February.

SCI-TECH IN REVIEW

Karla Pearce, Editor
Giuliana Lavendel, Associate Editor

READING EASE OF JOURNALS

Bottle, Robert T.; Tefki, Chaffai. Readability of French scientific texts. *Journal of Documentation*. 44(4): 339-445; 1988 December.

"Readability," based on an adaptation of the Farr-Jenkins-Paterson formula evaluates reading ease using a formula based on sentence length and percentage of monosyllabic words. The authors apply it to articles in three French scientific journals, *Annales de Chimie*, *Bulletin de la Societe Chimique de France*, and *Comptes Rendus de l'Academie des Sciences*. From this they derive a "reading ease value," which decreases as a text becomes more difficult to read. The formula is, of course, more complicated than that; presumably the goal should not be research reports told in one-worded sentences of one syllable. It was found that the *Comptes Rendus* underwent the greatest decrease in reading ease from 1835 when it received a score of 38.8 to 2.7 in 1980. It also has the longest sentences — average length increased from 29.3 words in 1835 to 35.3 in 1980. Incidentally, its sentence length peaked in 1940 with an average of 43.1, so at least that trend is a hopeful one. The author does not attribute this decrease in readability to the new polysyllabic terminology but rather to a wordier writing style. This trend is not limited to the French, as earlier studies have pointed out similar findings in English language literature. (KJP)

THE STEADY STATE JOURNAL COLLECTION

Dixon, Bernard. Science and the information society. *Scholarly Publishing*. 20(1): 3-12; 1988 October.

What has happened to the predictions of the paperless society? Not only have journals in paper not been replaced by electronic communications, their numbers have grown significantly, even in areas such as computer science where an online treatment would seem most attractive. An interesting discussion calls to question some widely held opinions on the use of scientific literature—for example, that browsing is still used as a research mode, and that currency of information in scientific periodicals is vitally important. Peer review is defended, while the value of conferences for information exchange is questioned. The author, who edited *The New Scientist* from 1969 to 1979, suggests some different solutions to maintaining your journal collection. (KJP)

ELECTRONIC LIBRARY INSTRUCTION

Caren, Loretta. New bibliographic instruction for new technology: "Library Connections" seminar at the Rochester Institute of Technology. *Library Trends*. 37(3): 366-73; 1989 Winter.

As testament to their technological awareness, the librarians at Rochester have revamped their traditional library instruction program to integrate electronic information sources. Even this presumably computer literate student population has members who are confused between floppy disks and optical discs or do not understand the relationship between the printed and online media. "Library connections" in a series of multi-media programs with chronologic segments, starting from a "humorous" depiction of early information retrieval techniques and services, moving through MARC records, shared cataloging, remote access, online and CD-ROM searching and finishing with varieties of document delivery.

Because of the modular construction of the seminar, its producers have been able to tailor segments to their viewer's particular interests. It has been very well-received, providing not only instruction in information access for their users but a forum for input from those users about their wishes for current and future library services. (KJP)

CREATING A SERIALS REVIEW LIST

Schmidt, Sherrie; Treadwell, Jane; St. Clair, Gloriana. Using dBaseIII+ to create a serials review list. *Microcomputers for Information Management*. 5(3): 169-182; September 1988.

In a project that started out as an attempt to manage a mandated 10% cut in their journal budget, library staff at Texas A&M entered their entire serials list of 15,603 currently active titles into dBaseIII+. Using codes which enabled them to compress records to a maximum size of 162 bytes, they were able to maintain an average input rate of 40 records per hour (their original goal of 60 proved to be too optimistic), thus completing the task in the alloted five weeks. After the collection development librarians added subject categories, price and other information, the lists were circulated among faculty members for recommendation to cancel or retain. In the end, about 7% of the journals were cancelled. This list has now become a "powerful tool for serials management" to be used for compilation of data, tracking of vendor performance, printing of binding and other lists, etc. This article also includes useful tables and a flowchart outlining the decision process. (KJP)

REPORTS ON JAPANESE SCIENCE – WHERE TO LOOK?

Stankus, Tony; Rossel, Kevin; Littlefield, William C. Is the best Japanese science in western journals? *The Serials Librarian*. 14 (1/2): 95-107; 1988.

"Japan has now surpassed all of the world save the United States in spending for scientific research . . . the Japanese (are) third in the world in output of chemistry, physics, and cancer research papers, fifth in general life sciences and seventh in mathematics." In light of this, should we cut American and/or European journals in order to add some Japanese titles to our collections? The author says no, because the best Japanese science will be in American and European, not Japanese journals. Defining high quality research by its *Science Citation Index* citation count, American journals publish the highest quality Japanese research, followed by those published in Western Europe. One must wonder, however, how much the language difficulty would affect these results. Included also are suggestions for testing this with your own scientists' citations to Japanese articles. A clear and useful response to the problem of rising subscription costs. (KJP)

THE NORTH AMERICAN SERIALS CONFERENCE

Strauch, Katina; Fugle, Mary; Markwith, Michael. Fatal assumptions: is there light at the end of the serials tunnel? *The Serials Librarian*. 15 (3/4): 117-131; 1988.

This entire issue is devoted to the 3rd Annual conference of the North American Serials Group, entitled Serials information from publisher to user: practice, programs and progress. This paper was taken from a panel discussion in which a librarian, publisher's representative and serial vendor discussed and questioned assumptions associated with the business of library serials. The librarian questioned the assumption that libraries should pay more for journals, even have to pay added charges with no apparent explanation. The publisher commented on the differences between serial and monograph publishing: a journal provides an entire field of knowledge, delivered in installments; and advance and other costs are much greater, usually taking five years to recover their investment. In what was possibly the most interesting response to the question, the vendor suggested that the librarian "drives the behavior of the publisher and vendor." He asks for a greater partnership among the three to manage and reduce the costs of doing business with serials. (KJP)

SCI-TECH ONLINE

Ellen Nagle, Editor

DATABASE NEWS

PASCAL Online

DIALOG is offering access to "one of the foremost collections of references to the world's scientific and technical literature." The PASCAL database, available as File 144, is produced by the Institut de l'Information Scientifique (INIST) of the French National Research Council (CNRS). It corresponds to the internationally known printed publication *Bibliographie Internationale* (previously called *Bulletin Signaletique*).

More than 8,500 journals are scanned regularly, accounting for 93 percent of the references. The remainder of the database comes from sources including theses, conference proceedings, technical reports, books. Patents until 1980 are included; biotechnology patents dating from 1983 to the present have been added. The file's principal subject areas include physics, chemistry, biology, medicine, psychology, applied sciences and technology, earth sciences, and information sciences.

PASCAL is international in scope, including abstracts in French, and controlled vocabulary descriptors in English, French, and Spanish (from a vocabulary of 80,000 terms). German descriptors are also provided for records on metallurgy. Each citation includes the vernacular title, and, in most instances, a French translated title.

For material added since 1982, an English translation of the title is also supplied. The composition of the file according to language of source documents is the following: 63% English; 12% French; 10% Russian; 8% German; and 7% other languages.

Because of the broad subject coverage, DIALOG considers this file to be "the premier source for information on virtually any science and technology field."

PASCAL began with approximately 800,000 records dating from 1986 to the present. The anticipated backfile will bring the number of entries to seven million records, dating back to 1973. Updates will add 40,000 records per month. Approximately 1,500 conference proceedings and papers, and 400 patents are added each year.

The price for searching *PASCAL* is $60 per hour. Print charges are $.50 per full record printed online or offline.

Health Devices Sourcebook *Announced*

A new online directory, containing current address and marketing information on the North American manufacturers and distributors of more than 4,000 classes of medical devices, is now online. *Health Devices Sourcebook*, is available from DIALOG as File 188. The *Sourcebook* covers all diagnostic and therapeutic medical devices and materials, as well as clinical laboratory equipment and reagents, selected hospital furniture, and systems and instruments used to test clinical equipment. It contains tens of thousands of trade names and more than 6,000 manufacturers, distributors, importers, and service companies.

The database is produced by ECRI, an independent nonprofit agency that evaluates health care technologies. Information on products and companies is collected and maintained by ECRI technical information specialists. Data are validated by mailings and telephone and personal interviews with company representatives. The *Sourcebook* file contains records verified within the last twelve months.

Health Devices Sourcebook contains approximately 8,400 current records. The file will be reloaded annually to revise existing records. An online thesaurus is included in the database as a guide to choosing appropriate product names and codes. The price for searching the database is $99 per hour. The printing charge is $1.50 per full record, online or offline.

Medical Instruments Database on BRS

The *Health Instrument File* is now available for searching on BRS. Produced by the University of Pittsburgh, it is currently funded by a grant from the National Center for Nursing Research of the National Institutes of Health. The database is a valuable resource developed to provide greater access to information about measurement instruments for the health and behavioral sciences.

The measurement instruments include questionnaires, interview schedules, observation checklists/manuals, index measures, coding schemes, rating scales, projective techniques, and tests. The focus is on instruments relevant primarily to professionals in medicine, psychiatry, psychology, nursing, social work, dentistry, public health, sociology, and anthropology. Instruments relating to all age groups are included.

The file covers instruments developed in 1985 and later, with some earlier, frequently used measurement tools included. Controlled vocabulary from *Medical Subject headings* and keywords from *The Thesaurus of Psychological Index Terms* can be used in searching. The *Health Instrument File* has a royalty fee of $20 an hour. Online prints cost $.40 for the full citation and abstract; offline costs are $.35 per full citation.

Toxic Release Inventory *on TOXNET*

The *TRI (Toxic Release Inventory)* is scheduled to become part of the National Library of Medicine's (NLM) TOXNET system in the late Spring of 1989. The file will contain industry data submitted to the Environmental Protection Agency (EPA) on the amounts of toxic chemicals released to the environment or transferred to waste sites. *TRI* falls under Section 313 of the Emergency Planning and Community Right-to Know Act, Title III of the Superfund Amendments and Reauthorization Act of 1986 (SARA).

Section 313, which mandates the *TRI* file, contains provisions for reporting routine or accidental toxic chemical releases to the air, water, and soil. This reporting of any of some 320 chemicals is required of facilities which manufacture, process, or use more than certain threshold amounts of the chemicals and which employ more than ten people. The law further required the EPA to establish and maintain a publicly accessible computer file, based upon this data. After examining various alternatives, the EPA decided on NLM's TOXNET as the system of choice.

The file structure of *TRI* is generally based on Form R, the form on which industry is required to submit *TRI* data to the EPA. *TRI* will be updated annually. The initial public file will contain submissions for the 1987 reporting year. An estimated 74,000 records representing some 17,500 facilities will constitute this first-year file. *TRI* users will also have access to the entire family of TOXNET files, including the *Hazardous Substances Data Bank* and other NLM files as well, such as the *TOXLINE/TOXLIT* group which contain 2.5 million references on literature related to toxic chemicals. Additional information relating to *TRI* will be provided in future issues.

NEW REFERENCE WORKS IN SCIENCE AND TECHNOLOGY

Arleen N. Somerville, Editor

Reviewers for this issue are: Laura Delaney (LD), New York Public Library; Isabel Kaplan (IK), University of Rochester, Rochester, NY; Kathleen M. Kehoe (KMK), Columbia University, New York, NY; Donna Lee (DL), University of Vermont, Burlington; Ellis Mount (EM), Columbia University.

ENGINEERING AND TECHNOLOGY

Dangerous properties of industrial materials. 7th Ed. By Irving Sax and Richard J. Lewis. New York: Van Nostrand Reinhold; 1989. 3 vol. $315. ISBN 0-442-28020-3.

> Volume one includes three articles on toxicology and carcinogenicity, and the indexes. Over 3500 new entries were added. The synonym index lists French, German, Dutch, Polish, and Italian synonyms as well as English. A Chemical Abstracts Service Registry No. index is also available. Volumes two and three contain chemical data and hazard potential for 20,000 substances. New features include structural drawings for selected entries and a notation that a material is included in one of several U.S. EPA lists. Clinical data on human beings and experimental animals have been updated and expanded. References for each entry are in the form of a CODEN abbreviation. The abbreviations are spelled out in the CODEN index in volume one. Except for the customary extensive use of abbreviations, this reference tool is easier to use than many catalogs of hazardous materials. (DL)

Directory of American research and technology 1989. 23d ed. New York: Bowker; 1988. 736p. $219.95. ISBN 0-8352-2478-3.

> Basic information one might need to contact 11,275 non-government research facilities in the U.S. and their subsidiaries is presented in this volume, which was formerly titled "Industrial Research Laboratories in the United States." Entries are arranged alphabetically and give address, phone, telex; names of top personnel, including the librarian; data on numbers and subject expertise of professional staff; fields of R & D; and codes to indicate parent organization, government or industry contractor, and consultation service. Data was obtained from questionnnaire responses. The *Directory* is also searchable on Pergamon Infoline. (IK)

Encyclopedia of environmental control technology. Vol. 1: Thermal treatment of hazardous wastes. Edited by Paul N. Cheremisinoff. Houston: Gulf Publishing; 1989. 827p. $135.00. ISBN 0-87201-241-7.

> The first book in an 8-volume reference series devoted to the problems of environmental and industrial pollution control. Examines current technology and research activities in the field of thermal treatment/destruction of hazardous and toxic wastes. Topics include incinerators and resource recovery systems, catalytic incineration of hazardous wastes, wood waste pyrolysis, and modeling of radiative heat transfer. Chapter references and a subject index provided. Appropriate for academic and research collections in environmental technology and hazardous waste treatment. (LD)

Handbook of industrial toxicology. 3d ed. By E. R. Plunkett. New York: Chemical Publishing; 1987. 605p. $75.00. ISBN 0-8206-0321-X.

> Data for at least 360 hazardous substances include synonyms, description, occupational exposure, threshold limit value, route of entry, mode of action, signs and symptoms, diagnostic tests, treatment, disability and preventive measures. Arranged alphabetically by common name, the information is provided in outline format to facilitate use as a quick reference guide. An index of substance synonyms aids retrieval. (DL)

Information sources in energy technology. Edited by L.J. Anthony. Boston: Butterworths; 1988. 324p. $105.00. ISBN0-408-03050-X. (Butterworths guides to information sources)

> A useful reference tool listing major information sources in energy technology. Divided into three sections, part one lists national and international energy agencies and services as well as primary and secondary sources of information (e.g., journals, indexing and abstracting services, etc.). Addi-

tional sections include information sources in fuel technology, nuclear energy, and solar and geothermal energy. Contains chapter references and an index to subjects, information services and organizations. (LD)

International petroleum encyclopedia 1988. Edited by John C. McCaslin. Tulsa, OK: PennWell Publishing; 1988. 388p. $95.00. ISBN 0-87814-327-0.

A detailed guide to the international petroleum industry. Broken down by country, this book lists statistics on petroleum production, refining capacities, and reserves as well as providing a good synopsis of petroleum activities in each country. Special features include an international active rig count, worldwide production statistics, world oil consumption data, and statistics on selected giant gas fields of the world. An excellent source for company information and industry statistics. Lacks a subject index. (LD)

Modern plastics encyclopedia '89. Edited by Rosalind Juran. New York: McGraw-Hill; 1988. 894p. $47.00. ISBN not available.

Published annually as the mid-October issue of the journal *Modern Plastics*, this encyclopedia may be purchased separately for use as a self-contained guide to the plastics industry. It includes signed articles on a variety of topics such as resins and compounds, chemicals and additives, fabricating and finishing, and design. A buyers' guide section provides an alphabetical index of companies including addresses and phone numbers and a classified index of products and services. A brief key word index and an advertisers' index are also included. (LD)

The radon industry directory 1989: everything you need to know everyone you want to reach. Alexandria, VA: Radon Press; 1988. 535p. $75.00. ISBN 0-929840-00-3.

A comprehensive reference source on radon-related information in the public and private sector. Contains alphabetical listings for several thousand organizations in the field including detection companies, mitigation firms, product manufacturers and distributors, research facilities, government agencies, and international associations. Individual entries include such information as agency title, address, phone number, key personnel, products, and services. A name index of agency personnel and an organization index provide additional access points. A useful reference guide for organizations and individuals seeking information in this rapidly growing industry. (LD)

HEALTH SCIENCES

The American Medical Association manual of style. 8th ed. Cheryl Iverson, Chair. Chicago: AMA; 1989. 377p. $20.00. ISBN 0-683-04351-X.

> Like most publishers, the AMA has always maintained notes on manuscript preparation and style for internal purposes. In 1962 they began publishing their notes. The manual covers the points of grammar, punctuation, and formats for references that any style manual would include. But this AMA manual also discusses concerns of particular interest to authors (and editors) in the biomedical sciences.
>
> The authors outline the steps in producing a journal, from peer review of manuscripts, to advertising, to makeup, to requests for reprints. The section on correct and preferred usage contains cautions on the use of medicalese and jargon. Half of the book is devoted to the correct use of medical and scientific terminology, including: abbreviations for clinical and technical terms, proper medical nomenclature, eponyms, units of measure, guidelines for use of statistics, and mathematical notation. Necessary for libraries supporting health care research. (DL)

Clinical pharmacology; a guide to training programs. 7th ed. Edited by Barbara Ready. Princeton, NJ: Peterson's Guides; 1988. 177p. $14.95. ISBN 0-87866-700-8.

> Aimed at residents seeking fellowships in clinical pharmacology, this guide covers 57 programs in the US and Canada. An introductory chapter presents an in-depth discussion of funds available for fellows. The main section is made up of individual entries for the 57 programs. Each entry describes the school's training program, clinical and research facilities, and sources of support for fellows in that program. A paragraph entitled "Representative Career Choices" highlights the current activities of some of the program's graduates. Entries conclude with a list of the faculty, their research interests, and a bibliography of selected faculty publications. For libraries serving medical schools and teaching hospitals. (DL)

How to find information about AIDS. By Virginia A. Lingle and M. Sandra Wood. New York: Harrington Park Press; 1988. 130p. $12.95. ISBN 0-918393-52-3.

> Since information on AIDS grows and changes so rapidly, the authors have wisely decided to focus on dynamic resources. Listings for organizations, state health departments, phone numbers for hotlines, computer databases, indexes, newsletters, and audiovisual producers make up the bulk of this handbook.

Health care professionals involved in AIDS research will already be familiar with most of the resources mentioned here, but laypersons and physicians in other fields will find the information helpful. (DL)

MASA: Medical acronyms, symbols & abbreviations. 2nd ed. By Betty Hamilton and Barbara Guidos. New York: Neal-Schuman Publishers; 1988. 277p. $49.95. ISBN 1-55570-012-8.

With over 32,000 entries, *MASA* (12,000 new entries) is intended more as a reference work than as a pocket guide. In addition to current abbreviations, the authors have included terms found in older literature and medical records. Anyone who comes across an acronym which is not listed in MASA is encouraged to call the telephone number provided so that the list may be updated. For all libraries containing biomedical literature. (DL)

Medical abbreviations: 5500 conveniences at the expense of communications and safety. 4th ed. By Neil M. Davis. Huntingdon Valley, PA: Neil M. Davis Associates; 1988. 139p. $7.95. ISBN 0-931431-04-2.

This pocketsize (4" by 6") guide is intended for people dealing with medical records, communications, and prescriptions. While the author has included all abbreviations that have been brought to his attention, he does advise that some of these abbreviations be avoided. Since these 5500 "conveniences" have 7480 possible meanings, the proper meaning must often be derived from the context. But even then confusion may persist. If a patient's chart reads OI, does that patient have Otitis Interna, or an Opportunistic Infection? In the preface, the author discusses some of the errors caused by medical abbreviations and urges the use of actual words (perhaps even complete sentences?) in communicating instructions for patient care. But as long as some people choose to abbreviate, the rest of us will need this book, or one like it. This particular list is less comprehensive than some, but is updated every other year. Recommended primarily for purchase by health care workers who want something small to carry around with them. (DL)

1988-1989 yearbook and directory of osteopathic physicians. 8th ed. Chicago: American Osteopathic Association; 1988. 697p. $38. ISSN 0084-358X.

The listing of Doctors of Osteopathy includes each DO's name, address, college, certification, fellowships, major professional activity, and practice area. Since the AMA recognizes the DO degree as equivalent to the MD, Doctors of Osteopathy are also listed in the *AMA Directory*. But this yearbook is more than a directory.

The Yearbook outlines the organization of the American Osteopathic Association, its philosophy, and its history. Sections on licensure, certification, predoctoral and postdoctoral training, osteopathic libraries, publications, research, and hospitals make this a comprehensive resource for osteopathy. Libraries which own the *AMA Directory* should consider purchasing this publication. (DL)

Varley's practical clinical biochemistry. 6th ed. Edited by Alan H. Gowenlock. Boca Raton, FL: CRC Press; 1988. 1050p. $79.95. ISBN 0-8493-0156-4.

This compendium of biochemical techniques, procedures, tests, instrumentation, and data is intended for use as a "how-to-do-it" manual for technicians in hospital laboratories. The 36 chapters cover such topics as radoisotopic techniques, electrophoresis, amino acids, plasma proteins, enzymes, lipids, porphyrins and hemoglobin, vitamins, and drugs and poisons. (DL)

LIFE SCIENCES

The biotechnology directory 1989: products, companies, research and organizations. 5th ed. By J. Coombs and Y. R. Alston. New York: Stockton Press; 1989. 569p. $170. ISBN 0-935859-50-0.

The first section lists international organizations, abstracting services, on-line databases, newsletters, and journals which cover any or all aspects of biotechnology. The second section contains entries for government bodies, national societies, and trade associations in 22 countries that deal with biotechnology. The third and largest section lists companies and organizations performing research and developing products. The authors have taken a broad definition of biotechnology, including industrial microbiology, genetic engineering and other aspects of health care, plant and animal breeding, waste and pollution management, and biomass energy systems. Includes an alphabetical index of companies and organizations. Appropriate for medical, science, and business collections. (DL)

Dictionary of microbiology and molecular biology. 2nd ed. By Paul Singleton and Diana Salsbury. Chichester, NY: John Wiley & Sons; 1987. $149.00. ISBN 0-471-91114-3.

This revised and expanded edition of the *Dictionary of Microbiology and Molecular Biology* is a well written, well organized work. It includes the terms, acronyms, and concepts which are currently used by researchers in descriptive microbiology, biochemistry, molecular biology, and bioenergetics. Some of the entries are limited to simple definitions, but many are encyclopedia length articles.

The authors have included a guide to the complex alphabetization scheme. This enables students to find the acronyms and biochemical names in the volume. There are also five appendices which contain flow charts of the most common biochemical pathways which have microbiological significance. Finally, the authors have compiled a bibliography of current writings for further reading. Although the dictionary's price is high, it is a must for research level biology collections. (KMK)

Encyclopedia of human evolution and prehistory. Edited by Ian Tattersall, Eric Delson and John Van Couvering. New York: Garland Publishing; 1988. 603p. (Garland reference library of the humanities; v. 768.) $49.00. ISBN 0-82409-375-5.

This encyclopedia is an excellent reference tool, and the only one of its type. It provides broad coverage of all of the facets of evolutionary and prehistoric hominid research-systematics, evolutionary theory, genetics, primatology, primate paleontology, and paleontology. There are over 1,200 (alphabetically ordered) entries. These are heavily cross referenced, and include references for further readings. The authors have included material to aid the reader in choosing appropriate subject terms, an overview of the content of the individual subdisciplines included in the volume, a classification of the primates, and tables of geologic time. The volume would be most useful to general readers, undergraduates or scholars from other disciplines.

Genome analysis: a practical approach. Edited by K.E. Davis. Oxford, Washington, DC: IRL Press; 1988. 192p. $54.00 (hardcover), $36.00 (paperback). ISBNs 1-85221-110-5, 1-85221-110-5.

This is a laboratory manual from the IRL "practical approach" series. It contains currrent protocols for the construction of gene maps, DNA fingerprinting, and related methodology. The authors are respected investigators who are proficient at the particular techniques they have described. Each chapter includes references for readers seeking further information on the subject matter. The volume was designed for use as a laboratory bench reference tool. It will be valuable in research level genetics collections. (KMK)

Insects that feed on trees and shrubs. 2nd ed. By Warren T. Johnson and Howard T. H. Lyon. Ithaca: Cornell University; 1988. 566p. $49.50. ISBN 0-8014-2108-4.

This revised and expanded edition of the 1976 handbook is a very useful reference tool for entomology and agriculture. The volume includes 900 species of insects which damage trees and shrubs in North America. Two hundred and forty-one color photographs are provided of species in the major families. These photographs are useful for diagnosing infestations — they show the insects at various stages of their life cycles and also show characteristic examples of damage to particular shrubs and trees. The authors have included a list of current pest control information sources and an extensive bibliography on the 900 species that help the reader with further inquiries. There are two indexes: one lists the insects in alphabetical order by Latin name. The other lists the plants which are hosts for insects in alphabetical order. (KMK)

100 families of flowering plants. 2nd ed. By Michael Hickey and Clive King. Cambridge, New York: Cambridge University Press; 1988. $79.50 (hardcover), $24.95 (paperback). ISBN 0-52133-700-3.

There are over 300 known families of flowering plants throughout the world. This book includes information on 100 represenative families and it is primarily concerned with plants which grow in the temperate zones. The following information is provided for each family: geographic distribution, general characteristics, economic or ornamental use, and classification. One or two representative species were selected and illustrations of the whole plant and its organs are provided for these entries. Several data tables are provided in the volume. These include tables comparing different characteristics and summarizing the presence or absence of different traits, among the families. There are two glossaries, a conventional glossary and a pictoral glossary which illustrates the terms used for leaf shapes. The book has one alphabetical index, which includes the names of the families and genera. This volume is not appropriate for reference level botany collections but it could be useful as a reference tool in public or college libraries. (KMK)

SCIENCE, GENERAL

Directory of technical and scientific directories: a world bibliographic guide to medical, agricultural, industrial, and natural science directories. 5th ed. Harlow, Essex, U.K.: Longman; 1988 (Dist. by Oryx Press) 288p. $95.00. ISBN 0-582-00602-3.

Formerly titled *Directory of Scientific Directories* (1969-1986), the latest edition of this useful reference work includes information on technical encyclopedias, dictionaries, and handbooks as well as covering national and international directories. The book is divided geographically and then subdivided by subject area (e.g., general science and technology, agriculture and environment, computer and electronic sciences, etc.). The approximately 1,400 individual entries include such information as title, author/editor/compiler, publisher name and address, year of publication, pages, price, ISBN, series information, and a brief contents note. Entries may also be accessed through an author/editor/compiler index or a title index. Recommended for sci/tech collections of all levels. (LD).

The guild handbook of scientific illustration. Edited by Elaine R. S. Hodges. New York: Van Nostrand Reinhold; 1989. 575p. $79.95. ISBN 0-442-23681-6.

A substantial reference work sponsored by the Guild of Natural Science Illustrators (GNSI). Covers illustration techniques in various media such as pencil, ink, watercolor, and acrylics. Supplies practical tips and suggestions on how to handle, measure, preserve, and draw a variety of subjects including plants, fossils, birds, mammals, amphibians, and reptiles. Provides a list of material and equipment suppliers and a lengthy bibliography. Beautifully illustrated. A useful reference source for any life sciences collection and an excellent handbook for the individual illustrator. (LD)

McGraw-Hill dictionary of scientific and technical terms. 4th ed. Edited by Sybil P. Parker. New York: McGraw-Hill; 1989. 2088p. $95.00. ISBN 0-07-045270-9.

The latest edition of this standard reference work continues in the tradition of its predecessors by providing clear and concise definitions of scientific and technical terminology. Contains over 100,000 terms with 7,600 new entries. Many of the useful appendices have been retained including the classification of living organisms and the biographical listing of noted scientists. New to this edition are the pronunciations following all terms. An invaluable reference tool for any sci/tech collection. (LD)

Pacific research centres: a directory of organizations in science, technology, agriculture, and medicine. 2nd ed. Harlow, Essex, U.K.: Longman; 1988 (Dist. by Gale) 517p. $300.00. ISBN 0-582-01608-8.

Lists approximately 3,500 industrial, government, and academic laboratories and research centers in Japan, the People's Republic of China and other western Pacific countries. Entries include such information as institution title, address, telephone number, telex address, affiliation or parent body, director, department or divisions, annual expenditures, activities, and publications. Includes an extensive subject index and a titles of establishments index. A useful reference tool for academic and research level sci-tech collections. (LD)

Science and technology annual reference review 1989. Edited by H. Robert Malinowsky. Phoenix, AZ: Oryx Press; 1989-Annual. 236p. $45.00. ISBN 0-89774-487-X.

>The first volume of what will be an annual series aimed at reviewing what the compiler feels are the best new publications in all fields of science and engineering. This could well be a very useful tool for those concerned with collection development in sci-tech libraries. Each item is given a rather extensive review, prepared by the reviewers, who are all librarians. This issue contains over 600 reviews, arranged under headings such as Agriculture, Medicine, Physics and Technology, then sub-divided within the chapters by headings such as Food Science—Dictionaries. There are four indexes—titles, authors, subjects and type of library for which recommended (although this particular index seems of doubtful value due to the overlap of interests of many types of libraries). All-in-all this is a welcome addition to sci-tech reference collections. (EM)

Writing for your peers: the primary journal paper. By Sylvester P. Carter. New York: Praeger; 1987. 129p. $29.95, ISBN 0-275-92630-3; $9.95 (paper), 0-275-92229-4.

>Intended as an aid to writers and ultimately their readers, this book is concerned with the function and organization of the parts that make up a journal paper: introduction, theoretical material, experimental material, opening and closing paragraphs, and credits. Unlike a style guide, it does not give rules for punctuation, drawings, tables, etc. Rather, it helps the author build a logical conceptual framework for the text. Notable are the three appendices which pose a series of questions which challenge the writer to examine and analyze his/her work from the reader's perspective. Recommended for academic and research libraries. (IK)

For Product Safety Concerns and Information please contact our EU representative GPSR@taylorandfrancis.com
Taylor & Francis Verlag GmbH, Kaufingerstraße 24, 80331 München, Germany

www.ingramcontent.com/pod-product-compliance
Lightning Source LLC
Chambersburg PA
CBHW070625300426
44113CB00010B/1662